THE BOAT'S GONNA LEAVE

Pragmatics & Beyond

An Interdisciplinary Series of Language Studies

EDITORIAL ADDRESS

Department Germaanse
University of Antwerp (UIA)
Universiteitsplein 1
B-2610 Wilrijk
Belgium

No. 1

Anca M. Nemoianu

The Boat's Gonna Leave:
A Study of Children Learning a Second Language
from Conversations with Other Children

THE BOAT'S GONNA LEAVE:

A Study of Children Learning a Second Language from Conversations with Other Children

ANCA M. NEMOIANU
University of California, Berkeley

AMSTERDAM / JOHN BENJAMINS B. V.

1980

ISSN xx xxx xxxx x
ISBN 90 272 2507 9

TABLE OF CONTENTS

1. INTRODUCTION

1.1 Purpose of the study

The purpose of this study[1] is to show *how* a second language is acquired by very young children in the process of socialization with other children. The study seeks to integrate the process of second language learning in the general framework of child development, concentrating in particular on the development of language and conversational skills.

Unlike most second language acquisition studies, the present study does not try to provide an outline of the course of grammatical development in the learner. In this sense it is not a typical second language acquisition study. It is primarily a conversation acquisition study. However, the second language is not only a prerequisite for the acquisition of conversational skills; it is acquired and developed in the process of conversing with other children. In this sense the present study investigates the first stages of second language acquisition by two children.

A second language can be acquired in a tutored or untutored situation, that is, in a formal, organized setting (the classroom), or in an informal, naturalistic setting (the family, the peer group). What characterizes second language acquisition -- as opposed to foreign language learning -- is the fact that in most cases it takes place both in an organized and in a naturalistic setting, with one setting complementing the other.

Children can be exposed to two languages from birth or the second language can be added later, after the first language is mastered enough to serve as a means of fluent communication. It is generally believed that children are by far more successful second language learners than adults, that up to a certain age they can add a second language to their mother tongue without much effort on their part, whereas adults, with very few exceptions, never quite attain a native-like fluency in a second language, no matter how hard they may try.

The present study is not going to dispel this common belief based on everyday observation and quite an amount of scientifically collected evidence. However, it attempts to show that the seemingly effortless acquisition of a second language by very young children is not what it appears to be: no matter how impeccable the final product may be, children differ in the ways in which they reach it.

This is an observational study of two German speaking children who learn English as their second language with the help of their age-peers outside the home. It is therefore a study of second language acquisition in an untutored situation by children who add to their mother tongue the "children's tongue", which is also the tongue spoken by the larger community in which they live. Two learning processes take place: learning to interact with age-peers and learning the language of the age-peers. The former presupposes the latter and at the same time represents the motivation for the latter to take place.

First, the study will describe the verbal interactions between the learners and an English-speaking child: how children organize the social situation they are faced with, i.e., conversation-play among age-peers. Second, the described conversation-play will be looked at as a source of language learning: what the children seem to learn out of interactions with other children. Third, the children's conversational strategies will be analyzed: how the learners put to use the linguistic knowledge they have.

The study assumes the centrality of communication in the language acquisition process. The second assumption is that children are willing and capable interactants. Language learning is not simply the result of observation and imitation. It implies *involvement*; in the process of verbal negotiation children feel the need to understand each other and make themselves understood, for the efficient use of language alone regulates their joint action. It may be here that the true motivation for learning a language lies.

It is shown that the strategies with which children approach conversation-play will affect the pace at which they acquire the second language, although they are still using the primary "mechanism" for language acquisition.

The present study emphasizes variation rather than uniformity in the process of language learning, without denying the existence of commonalities among children who learn a second language.

1.2 *Background: play, thought, language, and social skills*

Any study which aims at showing how language emerges in the process of communication between two or more children would have to at least tacitly assume that children do not talk for talk's sake, but rather that they are sociocentric by nature, that their talk is part and parcel of a more complex action which involves more individuals than the self.

This inevitably brings to mind Piaget's concept of the child as an intellectually egocentric being, unable to differentiate between his perspective on events and that of his interlocutors. Observing six- and seven-year-old children conversing in a nursery school setting, he asked himself (Piaget 1926) how much was real, meaningful, logical, "socialized" talk, and how much was monologue in the presence of an audience, random verbal support for action. A very large percentage of the children's spontaneous conversational contributions was found to be unadapted remarks (repetitions, monologue, collective monologue), that is, "unsocialized" speech. His study revealed a speaker who "does not bother to know to whom he is speaking or whether he is being listened to" (id.:32), who does not differentiate between self and others, who, although extremely talkative, does not have the *skill* and the *will* to effectively communicate -- a child who talks for talk's sake. According to Piaget, the child in the preoperational stage of development has this major cognitive inadequacy: he is unable and unwilling to communicate information or attitudes with a listener who does not have the information or attitudes he has.

Piaget's first and foremost interest has always been cognition, and only marginally -- given the position occupied by language in the child's life -- was he interested in the way the logic of the child was reflected in expressed thought. About his early work on child language Piaget later said: "Oh, my errors. I believed in language too much. I had the children talk instead of experiment." (Evans 1973). Naturally, he was disappointed to find out that "up to a certain age (we may safely admit that) children think and act more egocentrically than adults, that *they share each other's intellectual life less than we do.*" (Piaget 1926: 58; emphasis added). He did not look at children's conversations any longer, but chose to support his initial observations with communication experiments which showed that, indeed, verbal thought is not communicated between children; not any verbal thought, though, not the type that would occur in everyday conversations between children, but whole stories with intricate logical structures. But even in these experiments children do not appear as unwilling communicators; their expositions are frequently accompanied by remarks which reinforce the image of a cooperative conversationalist: "You understand", "You see", etc. Piaget's further comment is that "if children fail to understand one another, it is because they think that they do understand one another." (id.:116). It may well be the case that children do after all understand one another in everyday interaction, and because they know that they usually understand one another they fail to realize that on certain occasions they do not successfully communicate something for which they are equipped only to comprehend. In the study of child language it has since been shown that knowing something to say precedes the ability to say it correctly (e.g. Frazer, Brown, and Bellugi 1963; Ervin-Tripp 1964). That is not to say that the child cannot be at times an egocentric conversational partner; he sometimes indulges in private talk where normally adults would not, that is, in the presence of a listener. Whether in such moments he does not differentiate between himself as speaker and any other people in the audiences as Piaget said, or whether he is "para-social" as Vygotsky (1962) characterized him, that is, unable to differentiate himself of his self-guiding speech from other auditors, remains an open question. Researchers mostly investigated the strictly private speech of the children, i.e., the speech produced in the absence of an audience, and correctly pointed out that it probably has as many functions as social speech (Flavell 1966), and therefore it would be pointless to analyze it as an undifferentiated kind of speech.

A number of relatively recent studies show that the child is in fact capable of genuinely social language behavior by adult standards. For instance, Garvey and Hogan (1973) show that children younger than Piaget's subjects use language not for the sheer pleasure of hearing themselves talk, but in order to achieve social contact. In other words they are *willing* interactants. The absence of highly intellectual conversations may be due to the fact that they are too busy trying to structure the social situation in which they find themselves. Keenan (1974) and Keenan and Klein (1975) argue that two- and three-year-old children are perfectly capable of coherent conversations which, like adult conversations, follow some very precise rules. For example, they adhere to the Gricean maxim "Be relevant" not only by addressing the topic at hand, but also by repeating and modifying the phonological and syntactic form of the previous utterance.

These and other studies point to the child as an emerging social being. Sociocentric from birth, the child has to learn the rules and conventions of everyday life.

There is growing evidence from child language literature that the intent to communicate is prelinguistic, that the child first acquires a rather complex non-verbal communicative system (Richards 1974), that in the one- and two-word stages the child seems to be motivated by the desire to communicate, and that children learn turn-taking in both verbal and non-verbal interaction very early (Lieven 1977). Several studies are dedicated to the emergence of understanding and control over different speech acts, from "primitive" ones (Dore 1973) to rather complex ones, such as directives (Ervin-Tripp 1974; Garvey 1975; Mitchell-Kernan and Kernan 1974), disputes (Brenneis and Lein 1977), or types of responses to questions (Dore 1977). A theoretical framework for the analysis of child-adult conversations is offered by Keenan and Schieffelin (1975); in their study the child appears as a willing apprentice in the art of conversation, as a deft initiator of discourse topics, as an eager attention getter.

It appears that one of the first notions the child acquires -- in the prelinguistic stage -- is that of addressor and addressee, a prerequisite for socialized speech. Scollon (1974) shows how a child actually learns her first language in the process of communication: the child acquires syntagms of the language paradigmatically, i.e., the syntactic structures ("horizontal structures") are learned out of verbal interactions ("vertical structures") on a certain topic. In the process the child builds up, constituent by constituent, vertical structures which are at first linked only semantically, by a common topic of conversation, but which gradually become syntactically marked horizontal structures. It appears ever more strongly that grammatical and communicative competence are closely related, in that the child does not learn a set of abstract grammatical rules, but rather learns them in direct relation to specific contexts in which they are used. As Hymes pointed out (Hymes 1974), one cannot speak of linguistic competence in the absence of social competence; a message contains grammatically appropriate utterances spoken in situationally appropriate circumstances. All recent studies in child language either provide evidence for or assume the centrality of communication in the language acquisition process.

However, it seems that the will to communicate and the appropriate linguistic input are not sufficient -- albeit necessary -- for language learning to occur. The student of child language and his main subject, the child, are faced with at least three areas of competence which the latter has to acquire and the former has to observe and describe: cognitive competence, social competence (social rules and communicative regulations), and grammatical competence. How do these areas relate to one another ?

Slobin (1971) speaks about the "primacy of cognitive development" over linguistic development. He supports his argument with an impressive amount of cross-linguistic evidence to the effect that the "earliest grammatical markers to appear in child speech seem to express the most basic notions available to the child's mind." (4). The child, in Slobin's opinion, exposed as he is to speech in context, must have both "cognitive and linguistic discovery procedures" available in order to attend to input, to decode it, and to express his communicative intentions.

When Bruner (1972) refutes the strong version of the innateness hypothesis (as put forward by Chomsky 1965), he still allows the child some "innate special features of human action and human attention that permit language to be decoded by the uses to which it is put." (2). Rather than investigating these "special features" which facilitate language acquisition, he looks at *action* as the real prerequisite. The fact that phylogenetically, as well as ontogenetically, the initial use of language is "in support of and closely linked to action" does converge towards the Piagetian theory according to which thought has its roots in action: "Language is not enough to explain thought, because the structures that characterize thought have their roots in action and in sensorimotor mechanisms that are deeper than linguistics." (Piaget 1967:98)

The previous discussion about action, cognition and language is summed up in Figure 1.

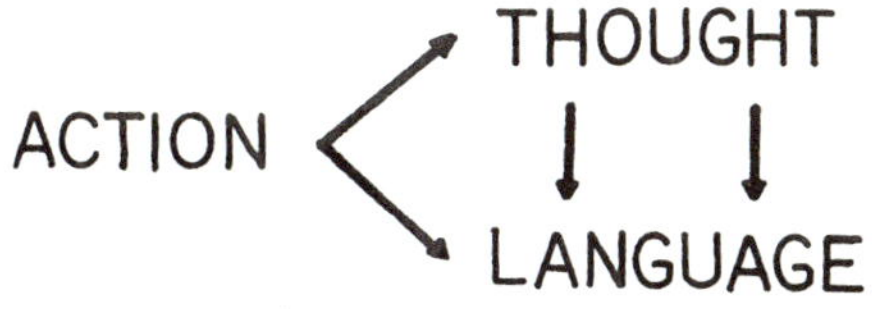

Figure 1. Relationship among action, thought and language

The kind of action children get involved in is *play*, not only solitary play, which most certainly contributes to their intellectual development, but also, and perhaps more importantly, social play. If we cannot speak of pure conversations between young children, it is because up to a certain age (perhaps into the period corresponding to the Piagetian stage of formal operations) play is the medium in which children discover the norms of the world they share with others. The sociocentric child discovers in play the structure of the interactions in which communication takes place. It is in play that cognitive, social, and grammatical competences are being shaped.

But whereas it is not easy to distinguish between what is linguistic knowledge and what is conceptual or cognitive knowledge, it may be even harder to distinguish the acquisition of grammar from that of communicative principles. Cook-Gumperz (1976), in an attempt to investigate how "the process of acquisition gets started through the shaping of prelinguistic social and semantic intentions and how language acts as a guide for further social development", found that two social principles guide the child from a rather vague social awareness into the acquisition of grammatical and communicative norms and regulations: the *reciprocity* principle, which implies that the child perceives other people as identical to him, and therefore the "language system of others" is "acceptable as an expression of his own intentions and understanding", and the *reflexivity* principle, which implies the awareness that language can control his communication with others. As long as he is guided by the reciprocity principle, the child cannot see the difference between his point of view and that of others because he depends on total reciprocity with them -- he has just one social rule for interaction. However, the child is not intellectually egocentric; he has not yet learned the other social principle (the reflexivity of language) which can bring him closer to what adults do when they communicate; he does not yet have the awareness that "all features do not contribute *equally* and *similarly* to the message".

Such an interpretation provides a larger framework for the analysis of language acquisition, which also includes a social dimension;

the relationship among action, thought and language can be thus enriched.

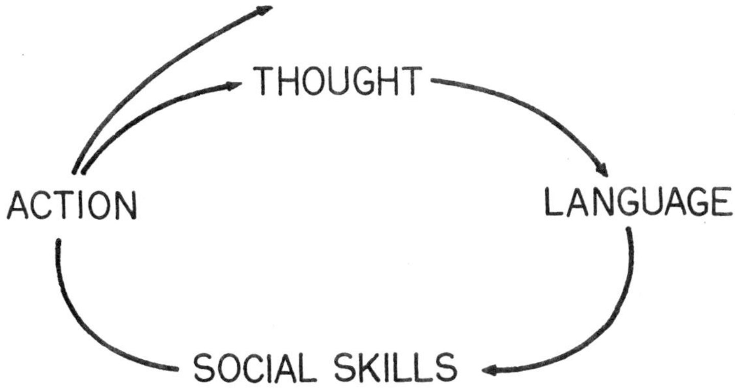

Figure 2. Relationship among action, thought, language and social skills

The relationship among action, thought, language and social skills is -- as the scheme indicates -- dialectic: the configuration is not a closed circle, but just a loop in the dialectical spiral of development. A quantitative gain in one area triggers, under normal circumstances, a similar gain in another area; periodically, such quantitative gains lead to a qualitative, i.e., developmental leap. Thus, an interpreted aspect of the environment, that is, a gain in the area of cognition, will bring about a better grasp of a particular linguistic area, which, in turn, may enrich social interaction and lead to higher forms of interaction.

We still do not have an answer to the old problem of the "starting point" in language learning; it remains a philosophical problem. In the debate between the cognitive determinism position and the language input position, a more moderate position seems to make more sense: a modicum of cognitive development must obviously precede any verbal or non-verbal interaction, since it is hard to imagine an interaction of any form in the absence of any form of knowledge, no matter how "primitive", about the environment.

In the situation in which a second language is added to the first one at an age when the child already has a good grasp of his first language and of his environment one does not have to be overly concerned with the problem of cognitive prerequisites for second language acquisition: the child has already discovered several aspects of his environment and has developed a method for further discovery. When children learn a second language from "conversations" with other children when they start playing with their age-peers, therefore when they are faced with two major tasks simultaneously -- a social and a linguistic task -- these are the two areas that deserve more careful investigation.

Inspired by the ethnomethodologists' work on American adult conversation structure, child language researchers have recently started to look at children's conversations, at such features of their conversations as turn-taking, initiating moves, and conversational repairs. Thus, Ervin-Tripp (1978) points out that, as far as children's turn-taking is concerned, one cannot speak about "intrinsic motivation for listening to all utterances, independent of all possible motivations, such as interest and politeness" in the same way in which the ethnomethodologists (e.g., Sacks et al. 1974) speak about adult conversation. One should rather speak about *interest* in the partner's conversational contribution and interest to participate in the talk organized by others, as well as about processing skills, in that a conversational turn which overtaxes the child's cognitive power makes him pay less attention to the norms of turn-taking observed by adults.

As to children's initiating moves in conversation, McTear (1977), who based his analysis on Sinclair and Coulthard's analysis of classroom interaction (Sinclair and Coulthard 1975), found that certain moves do not necessarily function according to the Schegloffian adjacency pair pattern, in that they do not require non-terminality, but can be terminal, that is, speaker A, the initiator of the verbal interaction, can legitimately shift the topic after speaker B's response.

During a conversational misunderstanding one important technique of self-repair was found to be the recasting of the same sentence in different word-order molds.

These studies analyzed child-child conversations from the point of view of the adult model or of models derived from the analysis of interactions among older children in formal settings, assuming that children's conversational behavior is nothing more than an attempt to approximate adult conversations.

In the present study the analysis of children's conversations will resort as infrequently as possible to the adult model as described by the ethnomethodologists; this is instead an attempt to "discover" how children organize dyadic face-to-face interactions and to describe the "structure of intersubjectivity" between the participants in the conversation, that is, "the mutual recognition of certain kinds of intention". (Ryan 1974). Although certain development features will be revealed, at no time is the assumption made that the conversational behavior of young children contains certain features which are gradually dropped in favor of more "elaborated" ones.

1.3 Conversation, play, and second language acquisition

Second language acquisition studies, with few exceptions, can be said to faithfully follow the more or less clear tracks left by first language acquisition research. The recent developments in the study of child discourse, more particularly Scollon's study, as well as the observation that children learn a second language "in the street", have shifted the study of second language acquisition towards discourse analysis. In other words, the emphasis has been shifted from *what* is acquired to *how* it is acquired. Children do not learn a second language by observing how other children speak, just as they do not learn their first language by listening to television (Sachs and Johnson 1972) or overhearing language. Non-personal language input is not enough for language learning to occur; it takes at least two to set the mechanism working.

In the field of second language acquisition research, while much has been said about motivation (Lambert and Gardner 1972; Schumann 1972), it is only recently that a study has shown that successful second language acquisition by children is a direct result of willingness to interact socially, that language learning evolves out of learning how to carry on conversations (Fillmore 1976). In Fillmore's study some of the first second language structures acquired by the children are precisely those which ensure their entrance into a conversation-play with their age-peers, and keep it going (e.g., "Lookit", "Wait a minute", "My turn", etc.). Those children who embarked upon the task of learning the second language with the primary motivation of making friends, of establishing an efficient conversational relation with their age-peers, deciphered the intricacies of the second language faster and with less effort than those who approached it as a task in itself, who thought before they leapt.

Hatch (1978) builds a case for the study of conversation in second language acquisition based on the premise that "language learning evolves *out of* learning how to carry on conversations." Looking at data from a number of older studies she suggests that puzzling problems can be clarified by analyzing the same data from a discourse analysis angle. For instance, the rather frequent construction "this+++NOUN", with falling intonation on each word, is not meant to be a random identification of objects or learning of names; if one looks at the following line in the verbal interaction, it appears that the interlocutor does not take it as such either, but rather as a topic nomination which requires comment.

Along the lines advanced by Hatch, Peck (1977) analyzes child-child interaction as a potential source of second language acquisition. In order to analyze the conversations between her seven-year-old subjects, she divided their language into language play, language during play, and language during non-play, and underlined the aspects of grammar that seemed to be practiced more in one form of language than the other. Whereas Fillmore's is a full-fledged language acquisition study, in that it provides an original explanation of the stages in which language is processed by the learner, it is not clear at the present moment just how discourse analysis oriented studies will handle the rule acquisition aspect, i.e., *what* is learned in the process of interaction. The morpheme acquisition studies (e.g., Dulay and Burt 1974; Hakuta 1974) have emphasized what is learned and the order in which *forms* are acquired. Next the emphasis was laid on the *functions* of grammatical forms (e.g., Gough 1975). The study of forms and functions covers what is actually learned in the process of second language acquisition.

The ambition of the second language acquisition studies based on a discourse analysis approach is to encompass both form and function and the *process* by which they are acquired. In order to do so the investigator has to describe *movement*, he has to describe the conversation, the process in which language is used and hopefully learned. He also has to observe how children handle the conversation, how they approach it, how much initiative they display, how they improve their conversational fluency.When improvement is noticed the investigator has to "freeze" the frame, and the synptoms of improvement have to be analyzed. What the discourse analysis approach to second language learning intends to do is to explain how language is used in communication, how grammatical form and function are learned in the process of learning conversational form and function. The approach foregrounds the basic idea that language is a major means of communication, and that communication is a social dynamic process, an idea which until recently seemed too obvious to be considered in language acquisition research. Nobody denied it, but nobody seems to have taken it seriously either.

1.4 Why conversation-play ?

Students of child language have looked at play and its role in child-child discourse and the acquisition of language. Cook-Gumperz and Gumperz (1976) point out the importance of the whole context of the speech event in interpreting child language. Garvey (1977) speaks about a general category of play which can be identified by the "key" of the speech event, that is, by the playful spirit and orientation in which the event is carried on. In so doing, she includes in this category play with noises and sounds, play with the linguistic system ("the repetition and variation of newly learned structures are believed to contribute to the child's developing mastery of his language"), as well as spontaneous rhyming and word play, play with fantasy and nonsense, play with speech acts and discourse conventions. Others make the distinction between different types of play and, as a rule, separate role-playing -- what Garvey calls "language in the service of make-believe" -- as a quite different type of play, conducted according to specific rules, which may not apply to other types of play. In the study of language acquisition, special emphasis has been placed on language play, i.e., play with the linguistic system at all levels. Fillmore (1976) shows that the most successful language learners in her study resort to frequent manipulation of language in a playful fashion, varying a theme they pick up in creative ways, be it at the phonological (sound play) level or at the level of syntax and lexicon. Language play helps them decipher sooner the formulas they initially learn as unanalyzed wholes. Peck (1977) shows how each communicative event contributes to second language learning. Thus, in non-play situations (arguments, "showing off") children make use of syntactically and semantically more complex structures. Language during play is the language which accompanies a game (e.g., a game of catch, a game of Mastermind, etc.); the fact that it is highly repetitive, she argues, may contribute to language learning through the practice opportunities it offers. Similarly, language play contributes to language learning through the cooperative or competetive "key" of the event and the practice opportunities.

Huizinga's (1949) older essay on play as a social activity and cultural phenomenon still offers insightful remarks. His definition of play runs as follows:

> "...play is a voluntary activity or occupation executed within certain fixed limits of time and place according to rules freely accepted but absolutely binding, having its aim in itself and

> accompanied by a feeling of tension, joy and the consciousness that is 'different' from ordinary life." (28)

If we look at conversation on the other hand and bear in mind Grice's conversational principles, as freely accepted but rather strictly binding rules, we can see the points of similarity between play and conversation. Their aims are different though: whereas play has an aim in itself, people do not normally converse for conversation's sake, but in order to exchange information, ideas, feeling.

Children do not talk for talk's sake either, but their conversation does not become focused unless it becomes conversation-play. For them play represents the entrance into the second language. The learners' primary motivation is their desire to interact with other children, at the play level, and since social play cannot in most cases occur in the absence of language, the gradual acquisition of the second language takes place in the process of structuring the play situation.

Bruner's claim that "the initial use of language is probably in support of and closely linked to action" seems to be particularly true in the case in which children learn a second language primarily from their age-peers. Since play and verbal interaction are so closely interrelated, it would be artificial to pull out of the discourse those instances when play is abandoned and conversation emerges pure and serious. It seems more appropriate to analyze the children's conversation-play. Laughter is not necessarily a marker of play; very often children play in profound seriousness. Also, serious interludes can occur in the middle of a playful episode.

It is not clear just how much is learned in play, but it is in play that some of the big questions about the nature of things are asked and sometimes also answered. Are we to point to a question like "Why don't lions talk ?" in the midst of a game with animals and say that with it the play stopped and a serious conversation was started ?

Furthermore, certain prosodic features which usually mark the shift to role-play may, with certain inflexible second language learners, be quite serious talk learned formulaically and reproduced the way it was first heard, as in the case of an adult second language learner who picks up an idiom from a Texan and shifts to a marked Southern drawl whenever he uses it in a non-Southern context.

Above all, in this study play is the context in which language learning occurs: the interactants, the setting, and the activity in which the interactants are involved create a system. In order to study the children's verbal behavior one has to look at all facets of the system simultaneously and at the various ways in which they affect one another.

For these reasons I will analyze the *conversation-play* of the children in this study.

2. DESCRIPTION OF THE STUDY

2.1 The subjects

The present study involves two children, Sean and Milvia, born in the United States of German mothers and American fathers, as they play and talk with an English-speaking child, Martin.

Sean was born in May 1974. His father is American, speaks English with his wife, and used to speak a little German with his son. His mother is German and speaks only German with her son. Between the ages of 1;3 and 2;7 Sean was taken care of by two German teen-aged girls, who spoke only German with him. His first language is definitely German. He started going to nursery school when he was 2;8 -- a private school run by a German teacher.

Milvia was born in March 1974. Her father is Japanese American, speaks English with his wife, and used to practice his German with his daughter. Her mother (and main caretaker) is German and speaks only German with her daughter. When she was 2;0, Milvia went to Germany and spent two months with her maternal grandparents. Like Sean, her first language is definitely German. When she was 2;10, she started going to the same school Sean was attending.

Martin was born in February 1974. Even though he is receptively bilingual in English and Romanian, he speaks only English, and therefore can safely be considered a predominantly English-speaking child. He is, compared to other children of his age, quite verbally mature.

Milvia and Sean had no peer interaction in German either between themselves or with other children.

The three children have known one another from the time they were 1;5, 1;7, and 1;8 respectively. Before I started recording their play sessions, I kept a diary of their language development. On all the occasions when the children and the mothers met in the park, the mothers spoke English among them, but the two German mothers spoke only German to their children and English to Martin. Milvia and Sean never spoke German to each other, as though they has not realized that they could fairly easily communicate in a language other than the one spoken by most adults and children around them. As a matter of fact, for a whole year they did not really play together: Sean was a solitary child, playing by himself for long stretches of time; Milvia clung to her mother, and thus German was enough for her; Martin would play with other children, at the same time trying to lure his German-speaking friends into his games. He soon picked up a couple of German words in order to communicate with them, but he often commented on their language as "baby-talk".

In February 1977, when the three children were 2;9, 2;11, and 3;1, they started playing together and actually communicating in English. Milvia and Sean started to pay attention to the language that had been flowing around them the moment their motivation was strong enough: it was as if they came to realize that the language they spoke, literally their mother tongue, could not help them have any meaningful relation with their age-peers, it could not allow them to become partners in play. They could not socialize with other children in their first language; neither did they know the language spoken by their peers. Once they started to interact with other children, the learning of a second language became a necessity.

2.2 *Data collection*

I started keeping a diary after the three children met, in November 1976, when the children were 1;5, 1;7, and 1;8 respecively, initially with the idea of recording Martin's learning of German. Martin was at the time eager to play with other children, and it was my expectation that he would "pick up" some German out of this contact.

But it soon became apparent that the two German-speaking children were not going to interact with him in German. At the same time, the two children seemed to be completely shut off from the language spoken around them. In fact, they seemed to be at the age when the only interlocutor a child needs is his mother or caretaker. The only English words they learned in a whole year were a couple of greeting and thanking formulas. Sean's German was "polluted" with the English adverb of negation, which easily took over at the expense of the German equivalent; Milvia preferred the English "thank you", and soon seemed to have dismissed the German equivalent as superfluous.

It took the three children over a year to start playing together, and then the language of communication was the societal language, English, even though two of them could speak German rather fluently for their age at the time. The two learners needed an extended "listening period" before they started interacting with their playmates in English.

In March 1977 I recorded their first play session, which took place indoors. I realized then that three children playing together could not be observed very closely: the dynamics of their play would have rendered a movie camera helpless, and, more importantly, one referee was not enough to settle their disputes. In the following sessions the children were recorded in pairs of two (Martin-Sean and Martin-Milvia). My presence as an observer in these play sessions has the disadvantage that an observer inevitably becomes at times a participant. Nevertheless, the advantage outweighs the disadvantage: the tapes could not have been transcribed without the detailed knowledge of the situational context. Most of the language recorded occurred spontaneously. But at times, I elicited words and utterances, not for the purpose of checking on the children's knowledge, but rather to suggest new topics during conversational impasses. The elicited speech was not included in the analysis unless it triggered a conversation between the children.

The setting of their interactions was one of the three playrooms replenished from time to time with new toys. Most of the toys were on shelves; for each session a number of toys were placed on the floor to suggest a topic for play: wooden blocks and a collection of small animals or cars; a train, adult dolls, horses; plastic stethoscope, syringe, telephone, ambulance, etc. Later, these arrangements became unnecessary: the children's later interactions did not require many props -- their fantasy furnished the setting.

The recordings were made on a Realistic compact recorder, model CTR-30, with a built-in condensor microphone. At first the recorder was hidden. However, since Martin was aware of its presence in the room, the secret could not be kept too long. His friends showed little interest in the machine; its presence did not seem to affect their behavior in any way.

The recording took place over a period of six months, from March to August 1977. In all, this study covers four play sessions of varying lengths (from 15 to 45 minutes) with Martin and Sean, and five with Martin and Milvia. Table 1 summarizes the analyzed play sessions; henceforth the participants will be referred to as O = Observer, M = Martin, Se = Sean, and Mi = Milvia.

In most cases the tapes were transcribed immediately after each session; contextual information was written down during the recording sessions. In addition to the speech samples provided by the transcripts, several samples from the diary were also included in the analysis.

2.3 *Conversation topic*

The method for analyzing the children's conversation-play topics used in this study was inspired by Keenan and Schieffelin's (1976) analysis of "topic as a discourse notion". Their analysis focuses on the way topics are handled in naturally occurring conversations, that is, the way they are initiated, sustained, discontinued, reintroduced, and finally dropped. A discourse topic is "a proposition (or set of propositions) expressing a concern (or set of concerns) the speaker is addressing." They analyze the discourse structure in terms of: a) topic collaborating sequences, where the topic is sustained over

SESSION NUMBER	PARTICIPANTS	TIME	AGE	SETTING	CODE
First play session	Se-Ma	Apr. 10, A.M.	2;11-3;2	Ma's playroom	1st PS/Se-Ma
	Mi-Ma	Apr. 25, A.M.	3;1-3;2	Ma's playroom	1st PS/Mi-Ma
Second play session	Se-Ma	Apr. 27, A.M.	2;11-3;2	Ma's playroom	2nd PS/Se-Ma
	Mi-Ma	May 6, A.M.	3;2-3;3	Ma's playroom	2nd PS/Mi-Ma
Third play session	Se-Ma	June 27, P.M.	3;1-3;4	Se's playroom	3rd PS/Se-Ma
	Mi-Ma	June 21, A.M.	3;3-3;4	Ma's playroom	3rd PS/Mi-Ma
Fourth play session	Se-Ma	Aug. 16, A.M.	3;3-3;6	Ma's playroom	4th PS/Se-Ma
	Mi-Ma	July 5, A.M.	3;4-3;5	Mi's playroom	4th PS/Mi-Ma
Fifth play session					
	Mi-Ma	July 24, A.M.	3;4-3;5	Ma's playroom	5th PS/Mi-Ma

Table 1. Analyzed play sessions

several utterances; b) incorporating topic, i.e., a new topic which includes information from one of the preceding utterances; c) introducing topic, i.e., a new topic which does not draw on utterances produced before in the discourse; d) re-introducing topic, i.e., a topic which reappears in the discourse. The first two moves (collaborating and incorporating) characterize a continuous discourse, while the last two (introducing and re-introducing) are typical of discontinuous discourse. Keenan and Schieffelin also point out the importance of *establishing referents* in collaborating on a discourse topic: "Listeners will not accept as given referents what they cannot identify in terms of general knowledge, prior discourse or present context." That is why speakers use all sorts of devices in order to ensure that the referents they are including in their topics can be identified by the listener. Sacks and Schegloff (1974) show that one such device used by English-speaking adults in order to ensure that their listener can identify the referent is rising intonation (e.g., ...Uh Mrs. Holmes Ford ? You know uh, the cellist ?). If the listener does not provide a positive response (verbal or non-verbal), this signals that he is not familiar with the referent, and further clarification is required before the topic can be established in a focused conversation.

At the age of the children in this study and in the particular linguistic situation in which they find themselves play and conversation stand in a very close relationship. Not only do the two learners not know enough language to carry on a conversation, but it seems that, at this age, they have the ability yet to engage in "pure" verbal interactions. Whatever the reason (limited memory span or insufficient productive knowledge of the language), they do not carry conversations longer than four turns unless they are accompanied by non-verbal activity. In other words, a topic becomes an established discourse topic only if the two partners are equally interested in it and try to "act it out". Non-verbal activity sustains a topic which would otherwise die away after a couple of half-hearted comments. The following is an example of a conversation between two children.

Se: ...A yo-yo. (holding a yo-yo) (= *Referent identification*)

Ma: It's not a yo-yo.

Se: What is *this* ?

Ma: A yo-yo, but it doesn't yo.
It doesn't have a string.

Se: I don't have a yo-yo. (= *Topic nomination*)

Ma: I do, but it doesn't yo.
It only goes like this.
(tosses the yo-yo and throws it away)

Se: (Picks up a letter box) Where is the
number on this ? the numbers. (= *Introducing topic*)

Ma: They are not numbers, they
are letters. (= *Referent identification*)

Se: Ye, I don't know letters. (= *Reintroducing topic*)

Ma: This is L. This is M.
L goes like this (traces
the letter with his
finger) /ʒ-ʒ-ʒ/ (= *Topic established*)

Se: And M goes like this
/ʒ-ʒ-ʒ/

Ma: O.K. I'll tell you how
H goes. (together)
/ʒ-ʒ-ʒ/

(*5th PS/Se-Ma*)

When Sean says "A yo-yo", he does not use rising intonation, but his mention of the word ("yo-yo") while holding the object in his hand can be considered as a way of checking if his partner could identify the referent, even though the object is located in the physical space shared by the two speakers. It is not an attention getting device, since the speaker has the attention of his interlocutor. When the referent is positively identified, the topic is nominated. However, the topic is not sustained because the toy does not function properly (i.e. it does not have a string) and, therefore, is of no interest to the children. A new topic is nominated directly. After the referent is clarified the new topic is established in play.

In a conversation between children of this age, unless the topic nomination is *Let's play with X* and unless it is accepted by both conversational partners, that is, it is of interest to both children, the discourse is mostly discontinuous. A continuous, focused discourse seems to emerge only if the topic is established in play.

2.4 *Situated and displaced speech*

One of the first norms of interaction the child learns, in fact well before he begins to speak, is the distinction between speaker and addressee. And among the earliest things he learns about communication are ways of getting the latter's attention.

The early conversations between adults and children have unique characteristics which are most unlikely to recur at any other time in someone's life; it is true that the child wants to communicate even before he has the linguistic means to do so, but it is also true that the adult is an extremely cooperative listener and interpreter. The child depends on total reciprocity with others because adults try hard to take the child's perspective into account as if it were their own. When the child reaches a point when he can effectively communicate with the adult who is most close to him -- parent or caretaker -- he discovers a new world in which the rules are different: the world of his age-peers. In this world a clash occurs between different perspectives; nobody pretends to take somebody else's perspective; the participants have to *collaborate* if the task is to be completed. That is not to say that children discover the principles and norms of communication in their world alone, that the amount of adult world observation is negligible. The observed norms undoubtedly play an important role in shaping their behavior, but it is only in practice, in actual interactions with equal partners that a real understanding of these norms and principles is reached.

Several are the metaphors that have been suggested by dyadic face-to-face interactions: a "ballroom dance, a performance improvised in process" (Erickson et al. 1973), "a three-legged race" (Dolan 1972), "feeling a rosary" (Erickson and Shultz n.d.) -- the cooperation of the participants is absolutely required. If during adult-child interactions it is the adult who takes care of any "stumbles" that may occur, in child-child interaction the participants are equal and equally responsible for their stumbles.

The two learners in the present study have an additional burden to carry: they have to learn the language of their peers as their second language. The social skills and the linguistic skills are learned at the same time.

The setting in which the conversations took place were the children's playrooms which were packed with toys familiar to all parties involved in the interaction. The choice of this kind of setting was based on the assumption that no significantly long interaction could be obtained in an empty room, since the children did not share the same everyday universe the way siblings do. The more general underlying assumption is that conversations between children, especially when they are unequal linguistically, will heavily rely on the physical context, so that the less linguistically competent of the two may have a chance to participate, i.e., to manifest his intent to communicate, to be able to interpret speech, to actually initiate and participate in verbal interactions.

Analyses of adult-child conversations reveal such a highly contextualized use of language by young children. The following is such a conversation between adult and child (Bloom 1973).

(Allison iv, 22 months)

A: (looks in box, finding calf) cow

M: A cow

A: (holding calf) moo/↑

M: Moo, cow says moo.↓

The children in Fillmore's study develop their conversations around toys and picture books. Peck's seem to use toys as a pretext for teasing the learner about the form of the language he uses.

When analyzing child discourse, one important aspect is the extent to which children make use of the physical context in nominating topics of conversation-play, in identifying referents, in shifting topics or repairing a misunderstanding. The speech tied to the physical context, which refers exclusively to the objects in one's presence, naming or describing them, and which is accompanied by the manipulation of those objects, will be called *situated speech*.

Children have to establish contact before a conversation-play is started. When they are on intimite terms, the conversation starts right away (e.g., Iwamura 1977, who collected natural language samples from two children who were good friends, on the way to and from school in the family car). Between children who are not so close, the social situation is not so predictible and, therefore, seems to require more careful structuring. The process of structuring the social situation, of starting a conversation-play of interest to both participants, of looking for a "worthy" topic, appears in my data at the very beginning of an interaction, as well as between episodes, when previous topics did not inspire the children with new, collaborating topics. Let us consider, for example, the following conversation between Martin and Milvia.

Ma: Do you know what Bert and Ernie have ? (with a rubber fish in his hand) They've got a rubber ducky. (Mi laughs) *This* is not a rubber ducky. (squeezes rubber fish) Quack-quack. (laughs)

Mi: (points to Ma's belt) This is a belt ?

Ma: Yeah, it's my Batman belt. You never saw my belt for a long time. You don't have a belt.

Mi: No. (both laugh)

Ma: Is this a tow-truck ?

Mi: Yeah.

Ma: Because it has a hook.

Mi: Yeah.

Ma: (with Batman) And this is the guy who has to drive it. Goes in the front. (sings) He's the driver. I can sing the song about

Batman. Would you like to hear it ?

Mi: (faintly) Yeah.

Ma: What is this ? Oh, your frog ! I recognize it. I knew your frog.

Mi: *Don't* touch that frog !

Ma: I used to have a sealion. (They got the frog and the sealion on the same occasion.) Remember that sealion ?
You were at Sean's birthday. Is this your toothpaste ?

Mi: No, that's not toothpaste. For my poo-poo.

Ma: (laughs) Ga-ga-ga-ga. (another tube)
Now what's this ?

Mi: Cream for my legs ...

(*4th PS/Mi-Ma*)

In sixteen lines of dialogue there is no real sustained topic of conversation; the two children search the physical space for things to talk about; a speaker identifies them (rubber fish, belt, tow-truck, frog, toothpaste tube, tube of cream), the addressee ackowledges his familiarity with it -- the whole discourse consists of short unrelated exchanges. The children laugh -- where adults would feel embarrassed -- but it is not their animated laugh that accompanies their more "serious", sustained, focused conversations. They do not feel embarrassed by their failure to establish a conversation: the wealth of objects in the room keeps the search for a topic going. The exchange is totally unfocused not because of the children's failure to take the perspective of the listener (cf. "Would you like to hear it ?", "Remember that sealion ?", "You were at Sean's birthday ?"), but because they have not yet found anything around which a mutually enjoyable topic can be developed. Turn-taking is strictly respected because each child wants to know whether the other one is interested enough in a possible topic for conversation-play, that is, if given an option the addressee will show commitment to engage in a conversation-play. Martin attempts to focus the conversation around Batman and the tow-truck, but Milvia's faint answer signals that he must try something else, which he does: "What is this ? Oh, your frog." This seems a very likely source of dispute. As will be shown later, in a coherent conversation on an established topic, Milvia's interdiction ("Don't touch that frog !") can trigger a very long verbal dispute in which each party brings arguments, marks his contribution prosodically (pitch and volume), more or less according to the stylistics of a verbal dispute suggested by Brenneis and Lein (1977). In this case, though, the topic is not established, and the child who is in a position to give a retort prefers to look for a more interesting topic. This "small talk" goes on for another nineteen lines.

Sooner or later, there is a moment in the verbal interaction when the referent, once identified, swiftly becomes the name of a game, and an established topic of conversation. At this age, a referent placed in memory (e.g., "Remember that sealion ?") can hardly play this part, I would suspect, because no play can be organized around it, except, maybe, in language play.

What makes a referent in a long list of referents suitable for focusing the conversation-play ? In the area of situated speech, a "literal" conversation-play can be started after several related referents have been identified: a car needs a driver, a road, maybe a bridge or a tunnel, etc. The action is so eloquent that there is little need for supporting language.

In the verbal exchange discussed above one referent identification triggers the convention of a more complex conversation-play. Once the topic appears interesting to both children, it becomes established in a game of make-believe. The situation is imaginary, and the objects in sight stand for make-believe objects. This will be called *displaced speech*. The way children can dissociate the literal meaning of speech from its situation is by pretending that the situation is different from what it really is, by indulging in fantasy assertions. This type of speech is in fact simultaneously situated and displaced: the language is "literal" in that it is tied to an on-going activity with objects from the physical environment; it is displaced in that an outsider can hardly make sense out of it unless he knows the underlying convention -- all the more so since children do not know how to mark conversational moves the way adults do. Corsaro (apud Cook-Gumperz and Gumperz 1976) noticed that children spend a great deal of time and effort and use various verbal and non-verbal strategies to start a conversation-play, whereas the end of such an event is often left unmarked. Before they know how to mark their make-believe conversation-play, children plunge into it directly, without any notice. The previous long list of referent identifications is followed by a make-believe conversation-play.

Mi: (near the bed) This my bed.

Ma: (running to the bed) The boat's gonna leave. It's almost leaving. Let's jump on the boat. I'm gonna jump on the board. (climbs into bed)

Mi: (Looking nervously around) Where's the baby ? (finds a doll, gives it to Ma) Here's your baby. (desperate) Emma, Emma.

Ma: Bye-bye. I'm going on the board.

Mi: No, you stay here with Emma.

Ma: Yes, I know, I'm tired.

Mi: This is Emma's bed. You are gonna drive.

Ma: Oh, I'm not gonna drive, I'm just gonna sleep.

Mi: That's not your bed !

Ma: No, that on the floor is our

bed. Good-night, good-night, Robin.

Mi: I'm gonna stay up, I'm gonna stay up all night.

Ma: You are not gonna stay up. Sleep ! (they both lie on the floor)

Mi: Close your eyes.

Ma: You close your eyes !

(*4th PS/Mi-Ma*)

Without any marking ("Let's pretend", "It's for pretend"), Martin projects the referent identified by Milvia into a fantasy world, where the bed stands for a boat. The rhythm of the verbal exchange becomes fast, both partners are very serious as they take off from the literal meaning of speech, even though there is no clear agreement between them as to the setting of the fantasy play. Martin's remark makes it clear that the setting is a boat, but he does not specify the identity of the characters: it is not clear whether he wants to be a passenger or a captain. Milvia does not seem to know the meaning of "on the board" (!), but guesses that Martin wants to be a boat captain, which she dislikes. Without any introduction, she changes the nature of the participants in the game: they seem to become mother-father-baby on a boat. The distribution of the roles is never marked in any explicit way; Milvia changes her normal pitch and intonation -- she sounds very much like a worried mother. Maybe there is a further understatement -- the baby is sick -- for she is ready to sacrifice herself ("I'm gonna stay up all night."). Martin understands his role by calling her Robin, an identity she usually assumes in fantasy conversations. The cooperation is perfect: each participant accepts the other's contribution and adds to it as the conversation-play develops. The conversation is cohesive, in that each turn presupposes the previous one, and the reference is textual, in that the understanding of each turn depends on the understanding of the previous one, and, more generally, on the knowledge of the convention of the play.

As Cook-Gumperz (1972) points out, learning a language is "more like learning to dance than like learning to walk." There is no reason to believe that learning a second language is different from learning a first language as long as the learning takes place in dyadic face-to-face interactions.

The two learners in this study learn the first steps of the new dance in conversations with their age-peers. At first their movements are awkward, but gradually more complex steps are learned, which lead to the mastery of the new dance.

3. FIRST STEPS

3.1 Routines in situated speech

In this chapter I look at routines as "predictable utterances that have a single or limited role, and are restricted to particular positions or specialized functions with respect to a conversation or interaction." (Garvey 1977). Such routines are usually conventionalized between interacting children; they are very close to what Fillmore (1976) calls "formulas", in that they are learned as unanalyzed wholes. The analysis of such routines may explain the great frequency of certain utterances in the learners' repertoire, and reveal the way they begin to be analyzed into their component parts, and subsequently used creatively in the discourse.

The routines discussed in this chapter are part of situated speech: they are means of referring to objects in the surrounding physical space, of manipulating them. At the same time, they play an important part in structuring the conversation-play.

In the early recording sessions the topics of conversation-play had to be suggested by the observer, who was in the same room with the children, or the children would find in the room a number of toys displayed such that the arrangement would suggest to them a topic for play. The learners knew too little English at the time to initiate a topic to their liking. The language mostly referred to the objects they were manipulating. Martin's early attempts at setting up a make-believe play went unheeded. The learners did not understand the idea of pretense: what was meant to be a make-believe conversation, often became a long and painful negotiation about the roles. This confirmed my suspicion that, because of the reduced linguistic competence they had in the second language, as well as the equally reduced ability to structure a play situation, they needed a prop around which their will to interact could gradually become ability to carry on a conversation-play.

One of the most frequently used routines was WHAT'S THIS/THAT. Until the end of the recording sessions, both Milvia and Sean dropped the third person singular copula in instances where it was required (e.g., "This you plate", "This my chair"). I concluded that the usage of the copula fluctuated not because the form was not acquired, but rather because of the difficulty of articulating two sibilants together (cf. "This your plate" vs. "It is my bottle"). The same difficulty is present in the utterance WHAT'S THIS/THAT. Nevertheless, the two learners did not drop the contracted copula in this case. That the learners used it a great deal was not surprising: it seemed that they were using it in order to request information about names of objects in their environment. However, Martin used the same utterance where it was obvious that he knew the name of the object. This suggested to me that the children were using the syntagm with a different function.

Holzman (1972) found that younger children learned to use the utterance WHAT DAT as three distinctive illocutionary acts: a) "I want to play the naming game", b) "I want that, give me that" (a devious strategy for obtaining a forbidden object), c) sincere request for information.

In the case of the learners in this study, one can rule out the third possibility as it applies to younger children who learn their mother tongue. They were familiar with the particular objects, they could point to them if they were asked, in both English and German. Obviously, there were instances when they sincerely requested information, not only about the English equivalent, but also about the identity of the object itself. In such instances, the utterance took a variety of forms, none of them correct (e.g., "What a dis ?", "What dis ?", "What is ?").

The question does not seem to be used as an indirect request, either; it is more likely that it is used with this function in adult-child interaction, if the child is perceptive enough to realize that the adult is eager to introduce him to the unknown world. As Ervin-Tripp (1977) points out, such indirectness is a rather late acquisition. The children in this study were very direct in most of their requests ("I want it", "Gimme that"), or would simply grab the object they wanted without any warning.

Likewise, the naming game is an adult-child game; when it is played by children, it takes the form of a ritual (e.g., the "you say X" ritual in Iwamura 1977). It is very unlikely that the linguistically more competent child in this study is checking on his interlocutors' knowledge of English, primarily because he is unaware of the fact that they are in the process of acquiring English as a second language.

The children in this study, in trying to structure a conversation-play, seem to use this question in their search of a common discourse topic. It functions as a conversation organizer, which can be used several times before a topic is established in a structured, focused play with toys and words. The question appears at the very beginning of an interaction or after a whole episode, during a conversational impasse, marking the fact that one of the participants is looking for another topic. Children seldom mark the end of a topic, but when they do it is mostly by marking the attempt to initiate a new topic: looking bored, glancing about the room, moving away from their partners. At the beginning of an interaction, when the participants are looking for something to do together, the question has the function of requesting indentification of a referent around which a topic may be established, in which case they have to make sure that the referent is correctly identified by both partners. As Keenan and Schieffelin (1976) point out, "the speaker should take into account the listener's knowledge or awareness of a particular object by making reference to that object within a discourse topic."

In the following conversational sequence Martin and Sean are searching for a topic.

Ma: I think I'm getting a chicken head. (giggles)

O : What ? (Ma and Se laugh) (O. pointing to the train displayed on the floor) Look here.

Se: Choo-choo.

O : Why don't you play with it, you two ?

Ma: (with a railroad sign in his hand) And I wonder what this is.

Se: That...

Ma: What ?

Se: What's that ?

Ma: (picking up a bell) And this is a bell.

Se: That not a bell...

(*3rd PS/Se-Ma*)

The search for a topic goes on in the following 26 lines of dialogue, where other referents are identified (bear, cat, frog, Mickey Mouse hat, water sprinkler, Batman), before a topic is initiated. Before it is established, though, the referent is thoroughly identified.

Ma: This is a train. (plays with the train) Chugga-chugga. What kind of car is this ?

Se: Hooo...Chooka-chooka.

Ma: This is a engine. This is a *engine*. These are all cars. And this is a ticket. Let's pretend it's gonna be (inaudible) time.

Se: Yeah.

Ma: Is this the station ?

Se: Yeah, is station.

(*3rd PS/Se-Ma*)

As a matter of fact, most of the third play session is a long search for a topic of conversation-play.

Ma: What's this ? A pencil holder ?

Se: Kooka, kruga...

Ma: This is a boat. No...it's a shoe.
It's a shoe.

Se: You can't take it out.

Ma: Can I swim with this ?

Se: Huh ?

Ma: People swim...Do you go
swimming every day with this ?

Se: Yah. In water, in a water...
(loud) I said in the water.
What's that ?

Ma: That's Batman.

(*3rd PS/Se-Ma*)

In all the above examples the two participants are facing each other, exploring the room together, eager to find an interesting topic for a focused conversation-play.

When a structured, focused conversation is consummated, at least as far as one partner is concerned, he is the one to look for a new topic, while the other continues to be involved in the old play. In such instances, the question WHAT'S THIS/THAT seems to function as an elicitation of noticing, like "oh dear", "ouch", "wow", only more powerful, since it is in the form of a request and requires a response.

(Ma plays with a car singing; previous
focused conversation -- a "pretend" play)

Se: What's this for ?

Ma: It's a tea cup. I'll give you some tea.

(*4th PS/Se-Ma*)

For Sean "What this for" is synonymous with WHAT'S THIS, whereas Milvia wants the referent identified first, and only afterwards does she request information about its functionality.

Mi: What's this ?

Ma: Oh, some batteries.

Mi: What's this for ?

Ma: For the tape recorder, but they don't work.

(*3rd PS/Mi-Ma*)

In a different setting, where there is no possibility to choose from among several possible conversation-play topics, the question WHAT'S THIS/THAT seems to be interpreted at first as the same old conversational move. Even though the addressee knows that the referent is well known to the speaker, he identifies it as he always does when the routine is employed. If the routine is modified, and the speaker asks for what Goffman calls a "re-run", this is a signal that the topic is established, this time in sound play, as in the following example.

Mi: (at lunch, picks up a slice of cucumber) What's this ?

Ma: Cucumber.

Mi: (picks up another slice) Uh ?

Ma: cucumber...cucumbi (laughs) cucumbus-cucumbus (both laugh)

Mi: (picks up another slice) What ?

Ma: Cucumbus-cucumbus capetti (laughs)

Mi: What do you mean ? (laughs)

Ma: Cucumbus cabetti.

Mi: Uh ?

Ma: Cucumbus-spaghetti, cucum, Milvia, this is *cucumbus*.

(*1st PS/Mi-Ma*)

In most cases the syntagm WHAT'S THIS/THAT has the specific function of identifying a referent for both partners in their joint search for a topic of conversation-play. When the form of the question is slightly modified ("What is *this* ?", "What *is* it ?"), the function it has is different. The speaker, who usually asks for identification of a referent in a perfunctory way, knowing beforehand the answer to the question, is puzzled by his partner's response -- the question is used as a sincere request for information. For example, when two children disagree as to the name of an object, they request clarification of the referent; they are reluctant to use a referent without information that the referent is known or knowable to the listener. In the following episode, Sean and Martin try to identify a referent in fifteen turns; even though the object is in front of them, they do not share the same word for it.

Se: ...Gimme that train. (Ma holds one car from the train; the rest of the train is displayed on the floor)

Ma: It's not a train.

Se: It *is*.

Ma: Uh-uh.

Se: What *is* it ?...It *is* a train.

Ma: No, these are the cars.

Se: No, no, no. That's a train. (points to the display on the floor)

Ma: It's a train, sure, but these are the cars.

Se: No, these are trains, (pointing to each car in turn) that's a train, that's a train, that's a train...

Ma: No, no, no. The whole thing is a train, but these are the cars and this is the engine.

Se: (gestures abundantly) This...is...train, that a train...

Ma: No.

Se: (angry, ready to start a fight) Yeah.

Ma: You sizzler ! No fightin' !

Se: Put it away ! Put it under your bed ! (throws the engine and cars away)

(*4th PS/Se-Ma*)

Garvey (1977) found that older children (5;2 and 5;7) ritualized insincere requests for information, which thus became material for play: the stressed *What is this ?* was uttered with "highly repetitive intonation and strict regulation of utterance and pause length." In my data there is only one instance where it is clear that the two partners engage in a "what is this" ritual; the ritual is triggered by the scatological implication of the answer, rather than by the realization that the request for information was insincere.

Ma: Is this your toothpaste ?

Mi: No, that's not toothpaste. For my poo-poo.

Ma: (laughs) Ga-ga-ga. (another tube) Now what's this ?

Mi: Krem for my legs.

Ma: (back to the first tube) And what is this ?

Ma: For my poo-poo. (Ma laughs)

(*4th PS/Mi-Ma*)

The speaker does not laugh when he asks the question, for that is not the object of play. The question is each time introduced by a different pragmatic connector ("now", "and"), which gives coherence to the ritual. After several disconnected remarks, the speaker resumes the ritual, which is this time understood by the addressee.

Ma: What this for ? (the first tube)

Mi: Huh ?

Ma: What's this for, I said.

Mi: For my poo-poo. (laughs)

(*4th PS/Mi-Ma*)

Although WHAT'S THIS/THAT is a rather prominent routine in the children's repertoire, they also have other similar routines whose main function is to identify referents for inclusion in a topic. IS THIS/THAT X ? seems to be a simple variation of the above mentioned routine.

Mi: Is this your big horse ?

Ma: Yes, it is a big horse and...

(*3rd PS/Mi-Ma*)

The same function seems to be performed by the simple mention of the word or by LOOK, LOOKIT, LOOK WHAT I FOUND.

Se: I don't see a horse. A yo-yo.

Ma: It's not a yo-yo.

(*4th PS/Se-Ma*)

Se: Look, look, look this car.

Ma: It's a truck.

(*1st PS/Se-Ma*)

Se: Lookit, lookit, what I found.

(*4th PS/Se-Ma*)

The children in this study did not seem to be able to identify referents out of the physical space during their conversations. In order to locate a referent in memory space several abilities are required both from the speaker and the addressee. First, the speaker has to mark the utterance lexically (e.g., *remember*) or syntactically (*past tense*), so that the addressee has time to search his memory for the particular referent; what may have struck the speaker as a memorable event in a past that they shared may not have been kept in the addressee's memory. Second, the speaker has to make sure that what he is going to evoke can be remembered by the addressee as shared knowledge; if not, the speaker has to make his contribution very explicit. Third, the addressee has to be able to travel back in time and identify it, and, if he does not have the ability to do it, to say so. Keenan and Schieffelin (1976) show that even adults find it difficult to identify referents in memory space, unless the speaker uses a salient trigger as far as the addressee's memory is concerned.

In an earlier session, two of the children, Sean and Martin, were playing with building blocks, trying to build a zoo for the animals. Sean is disturbed by the noise of a bus in the street and refers to it ("There is a bus") without marking the fact that he is talking about an object that is outside of the immediate situation. Martin, who apparently had not taken notice of that particular noise apart from other surrounding noises, tries to make sense out of Sean's utterance. He locates a like referent in memory and comments on it, unaware that that piece of information is not shared knowledge between himself and his conversational partner ("There's a bus down in the car", i.e., his bus had been left in the family car). Whereas the observer realizes that a breakdown in communication has occurred, Martin does not. He looks around for a second possible referent, this time in the physical space. This is accepted by Sean, but only after another unsuccessful attempt to repair the miscommunication.

Se: Let's build a mons for this lion.

Ma: There is no monster...

Se: There is a bus.

Ma: There is a bus down in the car.

O : What bus ?

Ma: (to O) The Greyhound.

O : No, he's speaking about a different bus. What bus, Sean ?

Ma: The Greyhound, the...you mean... Don't touch my cars. (Se tried to get a Batmobile) You mean (goes to the shelves with toys and gets a small double-deck bus) you mean this ?

Se: (points to his ears) De mude (?) here. (possibly: I heard a bus out in the street)

Ma: (to O) He means this. This is not a cage, it's a bus.

Se: (takes animal out of zoo, places bus in) Es is aus.

(*1st PS/Se-Ma*)

The initial topic is never resumed ("Let's build a cage for this lion."), although Martin tries to "straighten things out" ("This is not a cage, it's a bus.") Both participants in this interaction violated several conversational rules: one introduces a referent from outside the physical space the two share without making sure that the other can identify it; the latter pulls in a like referent from memory and introduces it into the conversation without explanation, thus violating the shared-knowledge principle. Later, Martin would mark referents from memory: first by *remember* plus a personal reminiscence (*I'm going to tell you something that I remember*), then by a comment in which he would reconstruct his personal experience in the past tense. Eventually, the lexical marker came to be used appropriately, referring to shared knowledge between the speaker and the addressee:

Ma: What's this ? Oh, your frog. I recognize it. I knew your frog.

Mi: Don't touch that frog !

Ma: I used to have a sealion. Remember that sealion ? You were at Sean's birthday.

(*4th PS/Mi-Ma*)

However, the two learners did not locate a referent in memory. Perhaps they were linguistically unable to comment on a proposition which referred to a past event. They seldom used the past tense, and when they did it marked a recently completed action.

3.2 Language learning in situated speech discourse

It is hard, if not impossible, to point out with any precision what children learn in the process of conversing with other children. Scollon (1974) raises the question: "Does the language develop because of increased social control of interactions or vice versa ?" And the answer he gives is a balanced "both things happen". In his study, Brenda, his subject, always had "the upper hand" in the interactions she engaged in. With visitors she was not allowed the same flexibility in structuring the social situation. The children in the present study are in a rather different position; their conversational partner is, in a way, like the visitors in Brenda's case: Martin does not organize his conversations around the learners' chance utterances and does not allow them complete control over the interactions. On the other hand, the learners want to engage in conversations with Martin and have to learn his language in order to do so. The social interaction is structured jointly; if one wants to control an interaction, one has to know how to use language effectively.

Fillmore's and Peck's language input providers adjust their language to the level of the learner, since they are conscious that their partners are in the process of learning a second language. In this study, the linguistically more competent child, Martin, expects his playmates to behave just like his other friends; they are not perceived as different from his other age-peers.

What do children learn out of their conversations with other children ? If they use a structure after having heard it, is this enough proof that the particular structure, as well as its functions, has been acquired ?

The learners in this study have inevitably been exposed to a variety of English input. It may well be that their comprehension of English was rather developed before they started to use the language productively, more so than in the case of an infant who acquires his first language or two languages simultaneously, and certainly much more so than in the case of most older second language learners. In the process of structuring a conversation-play they put to creative use the little English they have picked up along the way.

In situated speech discourse, in the process of identifying referents for inclusion in a topic of conversation, the linguistic challenge may not be too great, but the atmosphere is totally unpressured -- evidence of this is the fact that the process of identifying referents can take up to thirty minutes of a whole interaction. In this unpressured atmosphere several aspects of the language are practiced.

a) Deictic particles

Situated speech, that is, language embedded in the physical context, the language used as an accompaniment to action, represents an extremely economical code. For that reason, it is the easiest way of ensuring one's entrance into the second language and of establishing social contact with one's peers. The WHAT'S THIS/THAT routine may seem superfluous, since the object to be identified is in front of the children, they either hold it or point to it, and it is familiar to both of them. It is indeed superfluous propositionally, but it is a necessary discourse organizer.

The fact that each proposition is acted out with playthings could work against language learning since, the meaning of the event being very clear, the accompanying language may be very poor, lacking in both conceptual and structural complexity. In the case of second language learners, one could easily speak about the learners' avoidance to use language. But, once people agree that the most natural, logical way to answer a question which requires a locative is with a locative, rather than a full sentence, and that, furthermore, if the location is in front of your eyes, pointing to it is the handiest answer, there is no reason to believe that a child doing the same thing avoids speaking. In the following example, Sean does not avoid speaking; he uses language appropriately.

Ma: (trying to put a lion in the animal truck) My lion, it doesn't fit in.

Se: (opening the big door of the truck) In here.

In a situation in which the child has no other possibility to communicate his intentions than by resorting to language but prefers to keep silent, rather than struggle to get his intentions through, one can speak of avoidance. This aspect of second language learning will be dealt with in more detail when the children's conversational strategies are considered.

That is not to say, however, that situated speech does not have its challenging aspects, when one can speak about avoidance or involvement in conversation-play. Providing solutions for a "literal" game is such a challenging situation.

(after clarifying the referent -- the truck)

Se: Du lis dis open. (about the animal truck)

Ma: It's open, it's open.

Se: It has open de front.

Ma: See ?

Se: Put dem (the animals) in dere.

Ma: Animals...My little teddy. Hey, look what...he put something here and I can't look where it is.

Se: He's ja teddy.

Ma: No, I don't speak about the teddy.

Se: What...

Ma: About the thing that you bringed here. (Se had brought a little plastic dwarf)

Se: Dat's too littel.

Ma: What ?

Se: Letsee put here. (tries to push the lion into the truck through the front door)

Ma: O.K., O.K., you'll see. You'll see. This which doesn't fit in. Now it'll go in the big doors.

O : (about the dwarf) What's that animal ?

Ma: My lion. It doesn't fit in.

Se: In here (opening the big doors of the truck)

Ma: O.K....No ! (the lion doesn't go in)

Se: I think the big one. To dat door (in-audible) (the back door)

Ma: (tries, no success) No.

Se: Den back. Den backwards. I show you what big. I show you what...(tries and fails). No.

(*1st PS/Se-Ma*)

This episode, which occurred early in the study period, when Sean had very little English to communicate in, reveals him as a willing conversational partner, sincerely and deeply involved in the interaction. He is ready to investigate all the possibilities of introducing an animal in the truck. Had his partner been equally willing to try out all the possibilities, that is, had he been less skeptical, maybe Sean would not have had to struggle verbally so much in order to convince him; he could have played silently. The situation is rather complex and it requires urgent intervention. The utterances he uses are replete with deictic particles, underlined by pointing and acting. Deictic items are part and parcel of situated speech discourse, and the learners in this study use a variety of them (*this/that, in/over here/there, come/go, bring/take*), as well as notice verbs that accompany them (*look, see*), and extra-linguistic means (pointing, holding, etc.).

b) Lexicon

What children are exposed to above all else in situated speech discourse is a large number of nouns, mostly referring to objects in their world, accompanied by various qualifications and dictionary entries of sorts. Although it is not primarily a naming game, the WHAT'S THIS/THAT routine contains a large number of object identifications. In a conversation-play children spend a great deal of time in the presence of the objects about which they talk. This is, of course, the advantage of acquiring a second language in a naturalistic situation over learning it in the classroom. Children have a second advantage, namely the sincere and total involvement of their conversational partners, with whom they share the same kinds of knowledge about and interests in their universe. The comments they receive from other children may be idiosyncratic, but they may also be the comments they are cognitively capable to cope with. Besides, what seems a salient feature to a child may not be seen as salient by an adult.

Martin is an eager "lexicographer", or at least ready to provide functional definitions for the nouns he uses. The following are some examples.

Se: Who's Batman ?

Ma: He's the guy which has the thing on
his back that flies. He's a, he's a,
he's a man which has something on his
back to fly up in the sky with.

(*1st PS/Se-Ma*)

Se: What's a dis ?

Ma: It's an Exxon truck. It carries gas. Exxon trucks carry gas, don't they, mom ?

O : That's right.

Ma: (to Se) It's an Exxon truck and they carry gas. I like Chevron better.

(*1st PS/Se-Ma*)

Mi: What's this ?

Ma: Oh, some batteries.

Mi: What's this for ?

Ma: For the tape recorder, but they don't work.

(*3rd PS/Mi-Ma*)

The definitions may be more memorable to the learners than the comments they could get from an adult, since they are given in terms that mean something to them. However, they belong somewhere between situated and displaced speech, marking the transition from the verbal exchange which does not depart an inch from the physical environment to those conversational contributions in which the participants can be said to "share their intellectual lives."

3.3 Summary

Situated speech is highly contextual, where the word context is used metaphorically to refer to the physical context; it is characterized by what Halliday and Hasan (1976) call exophoric reference, i.e., reference to the physical context rather than to the accompanying text. It accompanies play with objects, the most common type of play children get involved in. Children in a reasonably familiar relationship, as opposed to the intimate relationship between siblings (Keenan 1976) or sibling-like partners (Iwamura 1977), need a period of "warming up", when they organize the discourse at the most general level, by identifying referents while in search of an interesting topic of conversation-play, which would be equally enjoyed by both partners. Naturally, they devote more time to referent identification when they are given complete freedom to choose a topic and establish it.

Developmentally, situated speech was used as follows:

a) In the earlier sessions, when the observer suggested a topic either directly ("Why don't you play with X ?") or indirectly (by restricting the number of toys and structuring them around a theme so that they would strike the children the moment they saw them), referent identification and the routines through which it is realized (WHAT'S THIS/THAT, LOOKIT, IS THIS X) occurred infrequently. In these earlier sessions situated language accompanied the children's "literal" games, e.g., loading a truck with animals, building a cage for them, building a tunnel, pushing cars through it, etc.

It is unlikely that in the later sessions, when the learners were linguistically more mature, their routines were sincere requests for identification of objects they had manipulated and talked about during their early games.

b) In the later sessions, when the learners had more knowledge of the language, were older and more experienced in socializing with other children, situated speech was mostly used for organizing the social situation. In these sessions they were given complete freedom to structure their interactions as they wanted. The greater responsibility was felt by the interactants, who devised routines to deal with the situation at hand. The identification of referents was used for two equally important reasons: first, the children wanted to make sure that a specific referent was shared knowledge, and second, they needed metacommunicative feedback, i.e., they wanted to check whether their partners considered the referent worthy to constitute the nucleus of a conversation-play topic. Thus, the same children who would jointly explore the world of play "because it was there" started to organize it very much as adults do, with the realization that "what's interesting to me may not be interesting to my partner."

In the process of manipulating situated speech in conversation-play, the learners were faced with rather unchallenging verbal situations, as far as conceptual and grammatical complexity was concerned. For second language learners this may be the best way to enter the "second world": cognitively adequate, the "here and now" language prepared the ground for the flight into the outer space of language.

4. TOWARDS CONVERSATION

4.1 Sound-play

Keenan and Klein (1975) point out that by the age of three sound-play as a mode of conversation is replaced by fantasy world assertions; both sound-play and fantasy world assertions are examples of displaced speech. On the other hand, older second language learners in Fillmore's and Peck's studies frequently resort to language play of all sorts, sound-play included.

The children in this study did not get involved in sound-play conversations, with one exception: the "cucumber episode" (1st PS/Mi-Ma, p.38-39) is a sound-play monologue, in that one child provides both the theme and the variations, but also a conversation, in that the addressee ensures the speaker of her attention and interest. The setting for the conversation in this study seems to be adverse to sound-play: the wealth of objects in the playroom suggests "meaning in action" rather than sound variation. When sound was played on it was in direct relation to an on-going activity; the "received onomatopoeia" (e.g., bow-wow, oink-oink, pow-pow) were modified in order to reproduce with more accuracy the sounds produced by the respective animals and objects in movement. Learning to handle a gun, for instance, includes learning how "it goes".

(Milvia picks up a gun and tries to shoot)

Mi: (gun pointed at herself) Sh-sh

Ma: You don't kill like that.

Mi: How ?

Ma: I'll show you. Gimme that gun.
Put it upside down, like this
(the gun faces Ma) and then you
go like this p^hju p^hju

Mi: p...p

Ma: No ! Like this p^hju p^hju (several
unsuccessful trials on Mi's part)
Yeah, gimme that gun.

(*1st PS/Mi-Ma*)

However, the accuracy of the imitative sounds is secondary to the action at hand. In the following example, the addressee is on the point of initiating a sound-play in the midst of a serious game and is rebuked for having violated the literal character of the play.

Ma: (starts a car, part of a "tunnel
and cars" game) Da-tsz, da-tsz.
(to O) I tell him how to start.

Se: Tsz-tsza, tsza (laughs)

Ma: Don't, don't be, don't be crazy,
Sean. Watcha mouth.

(*1st PS/Se-Ma*)

Their interactions are so much meaning oriented that even a very likely sound-play initiation (e.g., a German word which is not understood by the conversational partner) becomes a very painful referent identification process, as in the following example.

Mi: Have a Gummihose ? (= rubber pants)

Ma: What ?

Mi: Have a Gummihose ?

Ma: What ?

Mi: Have a Gummihose ?

Ma: What's a Gummihose ?

Mi: That ingoosh (?) (English ?)

Ma: Intosh ? No...You mean boots ? (goes into the closet to take his rubber boots) (Milvia follows him and takes the tricycle) No ! (puts the tricycle back into the closet)

(*5th PS/Mi-Ma*)

The fact that the learners did not initiate many sound-play exchanges has two possible explanations: as far as articulation is concerned the two learners seem equally inflexible and intolerant of sound variation; also the circumstances in which the conversations take place (a playroom full of toys) do not seem to encourage this type of play.

4.2 "Pretend" conversation-play

"Language in the service of make-believe" (Garvey 1977) or the language of role-playing is another example of displaced speech; the physical setting and the people populating it lose their life identities. More accurately, the language used in a "pretend" conversation-play is simultaneously situated and displaced; it is simultaneously attached to the people and objects in the immediate environment and divorced from the reality it stands for. At the basis of this type of conversation-play lies the convention that language is used metaphorically, that, for instance, if someone says "The moon is laughing at me" no one would reply that the moon does not have a face to laugh with. The child has to understand this convention before he can participate in this type of conversation-play. It has been shown that children check back during this type of conversation to make sure that the convention still holds, that what is said is still "for pretend" and not "for real".

For these reasons, "pretend" play represents a demanding language situation, in which the comprehension and production processes become more complex.

In the early interactions between the children in the present study few topics are handled in the "pretend" spirit; it is obvious that the two learners were not familiar with this type of conversation-play, which is an exclusive part of child-child interaction. The only recorded conversation among the three children was a long and painful initiation into this new kind of play: it consists of a thirty minute conversation in which the roles are negotiated. The least favored role, that of a baby, is impossible to assign because the spirit of pretense is not understood: Milvia does not want to take on another identity, she wants to be what she is -- a girl ("I wan be the...Mädchen."). What could have preceded the whole interaction occurs at the end, when the more "competent" player states the convention explicitly: "Let's pretend that you...". Still, it is doubtful that had the convention been stated at the very beginning it would have been understood by the children; more practice is necessary for the concept of pretense to be understood.

The processing difficulty is increased at times by the misunderstanding of the implication of the utterance, as in the following example.

Ma: (singing) I am the bad guy
and you are the good guy. (*Implication: fight*)

Mi: Yeah.

Ma: We're fighting. (= *Statement of implication*)

Mi: I don't wanna fight. (= *Implication denied*)

Ma: These are our guns.
(rolling up two place-
mats)

Mi: Ha ?

Ma: Yeah.

Mi: What ?

Ma: These are our guns.

Mi: What ?

Ma: p^{h}ju p^{h}ju (hands Mi a "gun")

Mi: What's this ?

Ma: Your gun. $p^{h}ju$ $p^{h}ju$ Let's fight. Burdiduki, yeaah. (hitting Mi with placemat)

Mi: (whining) Martin is hurting me.

(*1st PS/Mi-Ma*)

In the above episode the "pretend" conversation-play topic is nominated by Martin and, as far as he is concerned, it contains the implication of fight. The first misunderstanding arises from Milvia's acknowledgement of the proposition, which she seems to take as a real world assertion, and not of the implication that comes with it. The acknowledgement sets the play going, even though the statement of implication is not agreed upon. The topic is established by further complicating the convention of pretense: two placemats stand for guns. Milvia encounters a further difficulty, in that she does not seem to know what a gun is. Faced with two-fold misunderstanding, her only attempt at clarifying the entangled verbal situation is through a simple request for a "rerun", to use Goffman's term, which obviously cannot repair the basic lack of understanding. The complaint to an authority figure puts an end to an unsuccessful "pretend" conversation.

In later texts, the movement into a "pretend" conversation-play starts to be marked by formulas such as *Let's play X* or *We can play X*, where X stands for the new identity of the interactants, or *Pretend that X*, where X is a compound sentence which states the changed setting and/or the new identity of the interactants. The marking of this type of conversation-play does not always ensure its successful development. Before it becomes a routine which can later turn into a ritual, by a trade-off between explicitness and clarity on the one hand and quickness and expressivity on the other, the conversation-play has to be jointly shaped by the partners, both of them having to be equally interested in the topic in order to cooperate. The topic initiator cannot afford to be economical in directing the listener's attention to the topic; he has to convey it through several channels at once, propositionally, intonationally, and attitudinally. The following is an example of a "pretend" conversation-play between Sean and Martin.

(Ma -- when somebody is killed the detective uses binoculars to look for cues; Se has the binoculars) (= *Referent identification*)

Ma: Let me tell you something. Pretend that you were looking and he killed me. (= *Topic initiation "detective and victim"*)

Se: Yeah. (= *Topic acknowledged*)

Ma: Pow ! (falls down) (Se looks at him with the binoculars.
.....long pause.....

O : What are you doing, Martin ?

Ma: I'm dead.

O : And you, Sean ?

Se: Nothing.
(six turns around a new topic -- "a tea party"; only the objects with which they play are make-believe, the children keeping their real life identities)

Ma: (lies down again and pretends to be dead) (= *Topic re-introduced*)

Se: What are you doing ?

Ma: (slowly, with equal stress on each word)
I am dead.

Se: Why ?

Ma: Because somebody killed me.

Se: Who killed you ?

Ma: Roy. (a toy cowboy)

Se: Huh ?

Ma: Roy...Look at me and
then call the ambulance.

Se: (takes the toy ambulance)

Se: (continued) How come this
open ? (= How do you open it)

Ma: (shows him) Like this, Sean.
Sean, Sean, know what ?
I'll tell [you.

Se: [Yeah. What ? (puts
Roy on a white horse)

Ma: (angry) It doesn't go that
way. He (= Roy) goes on the
back of a black one.

Se: Where is the black one ?
(16 turns unconnected to
the initial topic)

Ma: (sings) Hey, Sean, pretend
that I got dead and you
called...the ambulance.
It goes like this. Pow !
(falls down) (Se comes near
him and falls down too)
You are *not* dead, *I*'m
dead. (= *Topic re-introduced*)

Se: My dead.

Ma: Pretend that I was dead
and you cal[led (= *Topic re-introduced*)

Se: [Yeah.

Ma: (Se picks up Batman)
That's not it (angry)
That's not the telephone,
this is the telephone.

Se: I want Batman. Can I
have Batman ?

Ma: (falls down again) Call

the ambulance ! You should call the ambulance.

Se: What can *they* do ?

Ma: They can get kids up. Right here is the telephone. Now call.

Se: O.K. (picks up the receiver)

Ma: No, first you have to do this. (dials the number)

Se: O.K. Hello ? (to Ma) He's not there.

Ma: I can tell them and then I go back dead. (takes telephone, dials number) Hello, ambulance (passes the telephone to Se) There !

Se: Hi, now are you ? Fine... Good. (hangs up) He's not there.

Ma: (calls again) The ambulance department ? Yes, they said yes. (angry to Se) Here ! Call the ambulance, the ambulance department, O.K. ?... I'm gonna call them. Hello, the ambulance department ? Yes. You are gonna come ? Yes. (lies down "dead") Ding, ding. That's the ambulance.

(*4th PS/Se-Ma*)

The topic of the pretend conversation-play is stated four times, and three times it is marked lexically by *Pretend that X,* where X does not stand for the new roles, which would have required further explication, but for the description of the pretend situation. The addressee acknowledges it; furthermore, he uses the object around which the topic has been initiated in the way stated in the convention of the play.

The implication contained in the topic -- the detective calls the ambulance -- is not understood by the addressee. After six turns unrelated to the initial topic, the topic is re-introduced. Speaking about discontinuous discourse and the way children fail to re-introduce topics or to understand re-introduced topics as linked to previous topics, Keenan and Schieffelin suggest that this is due to the children's short attention and memory span. As far as the topic initiator and re-introducer is concerned, the interludes are only means of luring the addressee into the "pretend" conversation-play.

The topic is first re-introduced non-verbally, then the gesture is explained slowly and clearly: the speaker reminds the addressee of the initial topic. What was not clarified in the previous section of the discourse (the agent of the killing) is clarified now, and the implication which will ensure the continuity of the conversation is brought to light ("Look at me and then call the ambulance"). The addressee, however, goes back identifying referents (the toy ambulance, the cowboy, etc.). The topic is re-introduced a second time; the identity of the actors is misunderstood by the addressee and, consequently, the topic has to be stated a third time. It is acknowledged again only to be carried out by the initiator alone.

The passage from situated to displaced language is full of obstacles and it requires a great deal of training before all these physical obstacles are removed and language can adequately serve the children's fantasy world. However, the harder the initiation process, the richer the language learning situation.

Along with a new identity, in "pretend" conversation-play the child learns different registers. Family roles are easier to play because the structure of the discourse and the registers of the actors are familiar to children. In fact, they are favored by children before the more distant registers of doctors, firemen, etc. The "pretend" conversation-play can develop more smoothly if the child is familiar with the role. In the following example, the convention is understood, but the addressee modifies her role into a more familiar one.

Ma: ...Hey, I've got a, I've got an idea. We can play doctors. This is a great idea. Great idea. I get the stethoscope. Where is the...Here. (gives Mi the stethoscope) You be the doctor. (He lies down) (= *Topic initiation*)

Mi: Are you sick ?

Ma: Yeah.

Mi: I have to call the doctor. (= *Topic acknowledged + role change*)

Ma: You *are* the doctor.

Mi: I have to *call* the doctor ...on the phone. Hello, hi doctor. Martin is sick because he didn't sleep. O.K., bye-bye. (to Ma) He works at the clinic tomorrow at one. The doctor's gonna come tomorrow at one.

Ma: Oh, after I take a bath. (= *Role change ackowledged*)

Mi: Yah, and you be good.

Ma: Yes, in the closet. (goes in the closet) Don't close the door ! (to O) We're playing doctors.

Mi: The doctor's gonna come tomorrow.

O : Oh, tomorrow. O.K., fine.

Ma: Good-night.

Mi: (goes to the telephone) Good-night.

Ma: (gets up) Today is tomorrow.

Mi: No, I have to call the doctor. Lie down.

Ma: Here's a boy and he had a
Batman with lemon eyes and
he closed his eyes, yeah.
(Mi takes Batman's cape off)
You've got it out. I'll tell
mom what you did. Mom...

(tells on Milvia, then goes
back to her)
You *are* the doctor. You
don *call* the doctor. You
are the doctor. (= *Topic re-introduced*)

Mi: Is this Batman ? (points to
a cowboy)

Ma: No, that's not Batman. This
is Batman. That is not Bat-
man in the car. Right here.

Mi: Police car.

Ma: No policeman...Let's pretend
that you are the doctor.
Just pretend. You *do* it.

Mi: (puts the stethoscope on Ma's
arm) Like that ?

Ma: (puts it on his chest) No,
like this. Now you hear the
heart go thump-thump. Ouch !

Mi: Pow-pow-pow (pretends the ste-
thoscope is a gun).

(*3rd PS/Mi-Ma*)

Here and elsewhere Milvia prefers to play mother for the simple reason that she knows how mothers talk -- this is the register she knows best. She seems to understand the convention of a "pretend" conversation-play, but cannot develop the topic when her role implies the knowledge of a register unfamiliar to her. Her proclivity towards the role of a mother/wife is so strong that she would resort to it even when the topic does not call for a change of identity or in a situated language exchange.

Ma: The boat's gonna leave. The boat's gonna leave..........

Mi: (looking nervously around) Where's the baby ? (gives him a baby doll) Here's your baby. Emma, Emma !

(*4th PS/Mi-Ma*)

(at lunch time)

Mi: Want some cheese ?

Ma: No.

Mi: Want cheesy ?

Ma: Yes, O.K.

Mi: Like cheesy ?

Ma: Uh-uh.

(*3rd PS/Mi-Ma*)

As a matter of fact, so present and vivid are the characteristics of mother (or, more generally, care-taker) register, that they can be triggered by simple gestures which in the child-caretaker relationship require and are usually accompanied by a reaction from the caretaker. In this study, Sean resorts to "mother language" in the presence of verbal or non-verbal stimuli which evoke to him alone a mother-child situation. These episodes will be discussed in more detail in chapter 5, where the individual strategies in approaching conversation will be analyzed.

4.3 Language learning in displaced language discourse

The language freed from the constant reference to things in the physical environment, from manipulation of things, the change of i-dentity and speech habits, the questioning of adult norms, disputes, are all forms of displaced language. Its meaning is referential: in some cases reference is made to the preceeding text, to a conversation-play convention or norm, to an attitude, rather than the objects in the physical environment; in the case of "pretend" conversation-play, one can speak about simultaneous reference to objects in the environment and the previous text, i.e., the convention that the things in the environment stand for something else. In Halliday and Hasan's (1977) scheme, displaced language can find its "place" somewhere between exophoric and endophoric reference, for, even though the language still refers to objects and actions in the strictly surrounding environment, these objects and actions stand for different entities, according to the convention of the game.

In the process of using displaced language, children gradually come to realize that they can use language in the absence of the things it refers to. With language they can do more than pointing to things and identifying objects, than expressing bodily needs and physical discomforts. These types of conversations are much more challenging both linguistically and socially. *The more complex the socio-linguistic context, the more challenging the learning process.*

What kinds of language complexities do children learn out of this kind of interactions with other children ?

a) Phonology

During the study the two learners had a rather strong German pronunciation of individual words and overall intonation. Their pronunciation improved considerably during the time when their conversations were tape-recorded.

In conversations between older children (Peck 1977), phonological errors are easily spotted by the more competent speaker, and could become the source of teasing and/or sound play. The linguistically more competent child in this study does not seem to consider his playmates any different from his other English-speaking friends; he expects them to behave, linguistically and otherwise, like him, he does not adjust his language to the language of the learners, he never resorts to baby-talk or foreign talk, he rarely corrects them, trying to make sense out of everything they say, e.g.:

Se: Let's go to d'anafan.

Ma: The animal farm he means.

(*2nd PS/Se-Ma*)

The most he does is repeat a form correctly, in a matter-of-fact way, which seems a very successful teaching method.

(Ma, Mi, O looking at a picture book)
O : What's he doing ?

Mi: uh-ʒumping

Ma: Jumping

Mi: Jumping

(*2nd PS/Mi-Ma*)

Teasing occurs only if the error suggests another word, as in the following example.

Se: (about sprinkler) It can puɚ. It can puɚ

Ma: (laughs) It can go poo-poo.

Se: No, it can, you can puɚ water with
it. (both laugh)

(*3rd PS/Se-Ma*)

From exposure and repeated usage their pronunciation is improved. Except for a very general intonation pattern (falling intonation on each word) borrowed from their mother-tongue, the two learners do not make errors that can be attributed to their first language.

One of the early errors -- the consistent replacement of the fricative dental /ð/ by the stop alveolar /d/ -- can safely be considered a developmental error: fricative interdentals represent a problem for young native speakers of English as well. Leopold (1947:112) reports that Hildegard replaced /θ/ and /ð/ with the supradental stops /d/ and /t/ in initial position, and with the alveolopalatal fricative /ʃ/ in final position -- "this is one of the most striking cases of substitution varying with position in the word, eloquent testimony for the difficulty of the sound."

Occasionally, Sean would replace the final English /ɫ/ with a vowel-like /r / -- hence Martin's misunderstanding of *while* for *wire*. The replacement of the two liquid sounds /l / and /r / in both directions does not come as a developemntal surprise: /l / has the feature that the breath stream operates over one or two edges of the tongue, whereas /r / "requires a complicated adjustment of the tongue muscles, which one could not expect children to learn early." (Leopold 1947:64). Like Leopold's daughter, Hildegard, Milvia would replace the initial /r / with /w / by rounding her lips: when /r / is followed by a rounded vowel, the lips are already rounded to attack the vowel. In medial position, she will altogether omit it and lengthen the vowel; this naturally produces numerous unsolved disputes with Martin, who wants her to pronounce the medial /r / in his name.

Most of these phonological errors are to a large extent absent in the later recordings. Undoubtedly, the suprasegmental problems will be equally solved before the children go to school.

b) Syntactic and semantic complexity

Whereas in situated speech discourse the emphasis was on the here and now and, consequently, on simple directives, requests for identification of referents, and what Dore (1977) calls "canonical answers" to such requests, one would expect more complex syntactic structures in displaced speech discourse, primarily because the possible misunderstandings are of a more complex nature.

It has been said that children resort to *juxtaposition* where more sophisticated speakers would establish more complex syntactic relations. In a dynamic interaction each turn contributes to the complexity of the larger discourse unit. Even though they are not marked syntactically, the utterances do not stand in a simultaneous relation to each other in the line of reasoning. Let us take, for example, the following stretch of conversation:

Se: ...He can fight cause he's Batman.

Ma: Yes, he can. He can fight bad people, not good people.

Se: We are bad, right ?

Ma: No, I'm not bad, I'm Robin, his friend.

Se: He can eat you up.

Ma: No, he can't eat you, he just fights bad people. He can't, he just eats food.

(*3rd PS/Se-Ma*)

Syntactically marked, that is, in an expanded form, this piece of reasoning seems to run as follows:

Se: Batman, as I know him, is a fighter.

Ma: He fights, indeed, but only bad people.

Se: We are bad, therefore he fights us.

Ma: He may fight you if you are bad, but not me, because I am his friend.

Se: Somebody has to be bad (according to my scheme of the world). Batman is bad and he will eat you up.

Ma: Since, as I said before, he fights only bad people and we are good people, he will not fight us. Besides, he does not eat people, good or bad, he eats food.

Even in the absence of any overt connector the argument is closely knit and it is understood by both partners, since in the end they are both satisfied with the conclusion. The juxtaposition of utterances with no overt gradation in development is the mark of oral cultures; the force of oral confrontation lies precisely in its lack of explicitness.

c) Pragmatics

"Pragmatics is the study of linguistic acts and the context in which they are performed." (Stalnaker 1972). The appropriate use of linguistic acts is most certainly the hardest part of learning a second language. It is equally true that no communication can take place in the absence of this type of knowledge. In child-child conversation what children seem to learn first is exactly the right usage of certain linguistic acts in appropriate contexts. They are exposed to rather limited style, the casual-intimate style used among age-peers.

What is interesting about the children in the present study is the fact that in their first language they have never and probably will never have access to this style. For example, they have never and will probably never organize "pretend" conversation-plays in their native language. They learn the second language because it ensures their entrance into a social situation where their first language seems of little use. Nevertheless, the verbal devices which organize their conversations are not qualitatively different from those used by adults in structuring conversations.

Whereas in situated speech situations children use mostly simple, straightforward directives *(Gimme X, Stop it, Put X here, Don't X)*, in displaced speech situations they start using oblique ways of ordering each other around.

One feature which characterizes a "pretend" conversation-play is the basic convention on which it is built. Once the topic is nominated (*Let's play X, Pretend X*), and the convention is clarified, the participants stop organizing the situation explicitly; depending on their knowledge of the register used by the character they play, the children are supposed to behave appropriately. For example, once it is made clear that one of the children is sick, the utterance "The doctor already came" (5th PS/Mi-Ma), spoken solemnly, with equal stress on each word, is meant as a directive for the sick child to enter his role. When the child fails to behave appropriately, his partner resorts to the explicit directive ("Lie down"); in such cases the "pretend" conversation-play may break down and the convention has to be restated.

Unlike the children in Iwamura's study, for whom one single word (e.g., "monster") conveyed the convention of a whole "pretend" play ("hide"), the children in the present study are still negotiating the roles and the appropriate behaviors implied in the new status expressed by the role. In most cases, such elliptical speech acts, which characterize the intimate style of conversations, are not understood.

The "boat episode" (pp. 29-30) is one of the few examples of complex events, when the situation is clearly understood from the very beginning, even though the roles are still negotiated along the way. "The boat's gonna leave" has a rather heavy intention load: the play starts, the characters are probably husband and wife, the tone is one of urgency -- if they do not hurry up they can miss the boat.

An analysis of the children's "why" questions shows the emergence of question directives (e.g., "Why draw on table cloth ?"). Ervin-Tripp (1977) points out that starting with the third year children use embedded imperatives (e.g., "Could you give me a match ?"), and the ratio of embedded imperatives to direct imperatives increases with age. With the learners in the present study the development of imperatives is somewhat different: at the beginning of the study the children used embedded imperatives, not because they were more polite than native speakers of the same age, but because the little English they had been exposed to was the English spoken among adults.

Se: Could have dis/dat ?

Mi: Could you the shovel ?
Could you...get out ?

These were the first formulaic expressions the learners had picked up from overheard conversations and among the first they used in their conversations with their age-peers. Their pragmatically inappropriate imperatives were met with annoyed compliance ("Sure, sure."). It was only after six months of exposure to and involvement in conversation-play with peers that the learners realized that there must be more direct ways of obtaining what you want.

4.4 Summary

The children in the present study use a lot of "language in action". Halliday and Hasan (1977) write that "if the situation is one of 'language-in-action', with language playing a relatively small and subordinate role in the total event, the text is likely to contain a high proportion of instances of exophoric reference", that is, instances of direct reference to things, as opposed to endophoric reference, that is, reference to the preceding text. In situated speech discourse children do resort to exophoric or situational reference. Not only do they constantly refer to things in the immediate environment, not only do they signal that reference has to be made to the context of situation, but they also manipulate the objects to which they refer, language being used simultaneously with non-verbal activity.

Displaced speech, on the other hand, is not synonymous with endophoric reference; it finds its place somewhere between contextual and textual reference, sometimes making simultaneous reference to both the linguistic and the physical context. It characterizes a transition phase from heavy reliance on situational reference to the ability to depart from the physical environment. That is not to say that child discourse is characterized by certain features which are never to be found again in adult discourse. Situational reference is obviously resorted to in adult life as well, in certain speech events maybe just as much as at any time in the child's life. But at the age of the children in this study and in the particular circumstances in which they find themselves (i.e., learning English as a second language in conversations with age-peers) situated speech seems to be used more frequently: it represents the entrance into the new language.

In "pretend" conversation-play a large part of the language is still "language in action", but reference is made both to the real physical environment and to the convention contained in the topic nomination.

The gradual transition from reference to the situational context to reference to a "pretend" situational context and finally to the linguistic context, the process of freeing the language from the physical environment is not an easy task. The grammatical and pragmatic complexities involved in the new language situation are increased. Evidently, the learners in the present study are cognitively ready to deal with this new type of discourse. What kind of impact does a more complex language situation have on a second language learner ? How does he behave conversationally when the language situation becomes more complex ? An answer to these questions will hopefully show *how* the two children in the present study learn English as a second language.

5. CONVERSATIONAL STRATEGIES

5.1 Argument

It can be argued that the more language children know, the more complex their conversation-play will *naturally* be. This argument seems correct: older children, who are cognitively and linguistically more mature, engage in more sophisticated conversations and games. However, if we look back at Figure 2, which establishes a tentative relationship among play, thought, language, and social skills, we can formulate the argument as follows, without being afraid of contradicting ourselves: the more sophisticated the children's conversations and games, the more mature their language will become.

Fillmore (1976) writes about the importance of social skills and strategies in second language acquisition, "because the learner must play an active role in inviting social interaction with speakers of the language, and also in maintaining the interaction once started." The strategies used in conversation-play are such social strategies. The key to success in second language acquisition -- as opposed to first language acquisition -- may lie in the child's "willingness" to communicate successfully, in his conversational strategies.

5.2 A matter of involvement

Piaget (1926), in his outline of the evolution from egocentric speech to higher types of interactions, distinguishes three types of arguments: 1) *quarrelling*, i.e., interchange of divergent opinions or desires accompanied by actions or promises of actions; 2) *primitive argument*, i.e., statement of divergent unmotivated opinions; 3) *genu-*

ine argument, i.e., statement of motivated divergent opinions. He also makes the rather surprising remark that "children between the ages of 4 and 5, although they are extremely quarrelsome, generally conduct their disputes without talking." By and large, there probably is a progression from quarrelling, to primitive arguments, and, finally, to genuine arguments; The final stage corresponds to collaboration in abstract thought, which one would not expect from three year-olds. However, as members of a rather strong oral culture, children do quarrel verbally.

As far as second language learning is concerned, I assume that language is learned not by mere observation, but by active involvement in its use. Verbal involvement implies both repetition of the interlocutor's utterance, repetition and expansion, and creative contribution to a conversation, on the one hand, and the refusal to accept a situation which is not understood or which is against one's opinions and desires, on the other. In other words, children can get involved in a conversation in a peaceful or belligerent way. Both are, in my opinion, useful learning situations. If the child is willing to actively participate in a conversation-play, he will look for and eventually find the ways to convey his opinions and desires.

We have seen that the children in the present study are willing cooperative conversationalists. The linguistically more competent child, Martin, is extremely sociocentric; he also has the advantage of knowing his conversational partners very well. He tries to make sense out of everything the learners say, does not correct them when their "errors" do not disrupt the flow of conversation. Neither does he make special linguistic adjustments in communicating with them. (His frequent unsolicited repetitions and expansions characterize his talk in general, irrespective of the listener.)

Neither learner displays much initiative in starting a focused conversation-play, but once it is started they behave differently. Sean can be a very patient observer for long stretches of time, complying with all the directives addressed to him, but contributing rarely, either verbally or non-verbally, to the conversation. He is not a particularly egocentric participant, for he is always attentive to what is going on around him and to his partner's talk. He would insert a relevant remark when nobody expected him to, as in the following example.

Se: ...And the lion goes up there (in the truck) And the lion goos up dere. And the lion goos up dere. Up dere.

Ma: No lion-goose. It's a lion. (to O) He said lion-goose.

O : No, he said the lion goes up there.

Se: Lion goos in the zoo.

Ma: Yeah, that goes in the zoo.

Se: Goes in the zoo.

Ma: Hey, let's build a zoo for that lion. Let's build a zoo, c'mon.

O : (to Se, who stares) You wanna build a zoo for the lion ? (Se stares)

Ma: You want to ?

O : (to Se, who still stares) Do you wanna build a cage for him ?

Ma: Do they like it in cages ?

O : I don't know, ask Sean.

Ma: (to Se) Do they like it in cages ?

Se: (absent) Yeah.

Ma: (to O) He said *yeah*.

O : You think so too ? Do lions like it in cages ?

Ma: Yeah, tell him.

O : Whom ?

Ma: Tell him if [he likes

Se: [You mean the lion ?

Ma: Does he ?

Se: He's not talking, you talk.

(*2nd PS/Se-Ma*)

Even though Martin seems to have lost hope of drawing Sean into the conversation, Sean was apparently involved throughout. Moreover, he seems to have better understood Martin than the observer. However, he is a cautious participant. He does not just leap into a conversation without thinking: unfortunately, this is a characteristic which does not apparently favor rapid language learning.

When he does get involved into an activity, the language barrier disappears, and he tries hard to put his thoughts into words.

(Martin tries to put the lion into the animal truck)

Ma: My lion. It doesn't fit.

Se: (opening the big doors of the truck)
In here.

Ma: O.K. (tries) No.

Se: I think in the big one. To dat door...

Ma: (tries again) No.

Se: Den back, den backwards. I show you
what big, I show you what ...(tries) No !

O : Well, maybe you can find a small animal
which goes in there.

Se: I find another animal.

(*1st PS/Se-Ma*)

In a more complex language situation, for instance in a "pretend" conversation-play, he keeps avoiding the main topic by interrupting his partner with remarks about objects he happens to notice while glancing about the room. For a whole recording session (e.g., 3rd PS/Se-Ma), he can move around the room identifying objects without becoming interested in any conversation-play topic his partner nominates.

He rarely contradicts his partner. One of their few verbal quarrels is started around the identification of a referent.

Se: ...gimme that train. (Ma holds one car from the train)

Ma: It's not a train.

Se: It *is*.

Ma: Uh-uh.

Se: What is it ? It *is* a train.

Ma: No, these are the cars.

Se: No, no, no. That's a train. (points at engine plus several train cars)

Ma: It's a train, sure, but *these* are the cars.

Se: No, these are trains. That's a train, that's a train... (pointing to each car in turn)

Ma: No, no, no. The whole thing is a train, but these are the cars and this is the engine.

Se: This is a train, that's a tr[ain

Ma: [No !

Se: (angry) Yeah (heading for Ma, ready to start a fight)

Ma: You sizzler ! No fightin' !

Se: Put it away ! Put it under your bed ! (throws engine and cars away)

(*4th PS/Mi-Ma*)

Brenneis and Lein's (1977) analysis of children's disputes confines itself to role-play disputes, in that the children in their study were given scripts which contained the content of an argument, and were left to perform the disputes as they thought appropriate. Nevertheless, their categories of content and stylistic tactics can serve as a reference point in a discussion of any child-child arguments.

In the preceding speech sample, Sean's initial demand ("gimme that train") could easily become a content basis for an argument. However, maybe in order to avoid compliance with Sean's demand, Martin negates only one constituent in Sean's utterance, rather than the whole proposition. The argument is started either because the listener tries to avoid compliance with the speaker's demand or, more likely, because they do not share the same lexical entry for the word "train": Sean does not make the distinction between the segments ("cars") and the whole ("train").

The argument proceeds along an "inversion pattern" ("It is" vs. "It is not"), which Brenneis and Lein call "the building blocks" of disputes between children. An apparent breakdown in the structure of the argument occurs when Sean asks for a reason for Martin's denial -- the correct identification of the referent. The following sequence in the argument is developed around the content of each participant's proposition ("A train is made of an engine and cars" vs. "A train is a train"). Stylistically, the sequence is somewhat atypical of children's arguments: Martin's turns are unmarked stylistically (volume, speed, stress), but contentful; Sean's turns are heavily marked stylistically, in that they are characterized by stress at first, which, failing to establish a rhythmical pattern with his interlocutor's response, is replaced by volume escalation and acceleration. The third sequence of the argument is again inversion ("This is a train" / "No"), which does not last longer than two turns because the argument has already reached its climax in the second sequence, and breaks down with a final non-verbal promise of action and an insult.

The only other argument in their verbal exchanges is formed along the typical alternation between assertion and contradictory assertion, rhythmically stressed, breaking down in conditional surrender.

Sean does not get involved in verbal arguments, even though he does tend to get involved in his share of controversy: he engages his playmates in combat. He finds it easier to question the authority of an interdiction than start an argument. In general, he prefers to observe how the social situation is structured by his partner, he marks the fact that he is present in the conversation by carrying out orders; he gives short, mostly affirmative answers to his partner's questions, even when the appropriate answer would be negative (e.g., *Do you know what X is ? -- Yes, what ?*), and resorts to responses which limit one's commitment to say more (*I donno*) as frequently as possible.

Another peculiar strategy he uses, i.e., intervention in a conversation with a "quotation", an automatic response to certain verbal stimuli, uttered with the intonation and voice quality of the adult from whom he first heard it -- will be discussed in the next section.

As far as involvement in a conversation-play is concerned, Sean meets challenge with avoidance. Consequently, he seems to learn the second language at a slower pace than Milvia.

Milvia, on the other hand, meets the verbal challenge head-on. An obstinate, unyielding personality, for her the language barrier disappears when she has to prove her point. When there is a battle of wills, she never gives in; she quarrels verbally until her partner gives in. She contradicts for the sake of contradiction and seems to be aware of it. She likes to tease and takes great pleasure when her partner gets caught in her trap, as in the following example.

(O, Milvia, and Martin "read" a picture book)

O : Where is she (the cat), Milvia ?

Ma: In the bed.

O : I asked Milvia.[2]

Mi: (smiling) Under the bed.

Ma: On the bed.

Mi: (smiles to O) *Unter* the bed.

Ma: I said on. *See ?* (points to the picture)

(*2nd PS/Mi-Ma*)

The more understanding her partner becomes, the more she modifies her desires in order to antagonize him, as in the following example.

(reading the same book)

Mi: That's my dog.

O : This is your dog ?

Ma: Yeah, and this is my cat.

Mi: That's *my* cat.

Ma: And this is my dog.

Mi: This all of my dog. (pointing to the dog and the cat)

Ma: No, I've got to have this cat.

Mi: I wanna cat.

Ma: I want the dog then.

Mi: I want this *dog*. (points to dog on next page)

Ma: These are not two dogs. That's the same. The jacket. (= the same dog with a jacket on)

(*2nd PS/Mi-Ma*)

The argument arises from a misunderstanding: Martin interprets the situation as meaning "sharing of goods", whereas Milvia wants everything for herself, and conveys her idea verbally ("This all of my dog.") and non-verbally (pointing to both pictures). Until they understand the concept of sharing, most of the children's arguments are caused by their strong feelings of possession; hence the frequent "mineing" (*It's mine* vs. *It's mine*), as Cook-Gumperz calls them. The stylistic pattern which characterizes this type of argument consists of assertion and counter-assertion, the latter with modified stress and increased volume.

(at lunch, fighting for chairs)

Mi: I want it.

Ma: She's moving *my* chair away.

Mi: That's *my* chair.

Ma: No, that's *my* chair.

Mi: I wannit. I wanna move this chair.

Ma: That's where my mom's chair is.

Mi: I'll sit over here.

Ma: That's where *I* get to eat. (screams)

Mi: This is your plate. (moves the plate to Ma's new place)

(*1st PS/Mi-Ma*)

Furthermore, Milvia rejects any directive that puts her into a submissive role, and is ready to argue it to the end.

(Ma and Mi do a squirrel jigsaw puzzle)

Ma: (Drops a piece of the puzzle) Stop !

Mi: What ?

Ma: Stop doing this, stop doing this, squirrel. (another piece falls) Now stop, stop !

Mi: Yeah ? I don't have to stop.

Ma: I said it to the squirrel.

(*4th PS/Mi-Ma*)

On the other hand, she enjoys ordering her partner around.

Mi: Go into your room, go into your room, go into your room. I can't talk, I can't talk. Can't talk.

Ma: Don't talk.

Mi: You *have* to go into your room.

Ma: Stop it.

Mi: Go into your room !

Ma: Stop ! Go in *your* room. Go inside and *stay* there.

Mi: (shouting) Noooo.

Ma: (sings)

Mi: Don't !

Ma: Shut up !

Mi: You shuddup !

(*4th PS/Mi-Ma*)

Such disputes are usually settled with an insult and promise of action or with a supportive assertion; when the supportive assertion is a strong motivation of one's opinions or desires, the argument takes the form of a genuine verbal argument. In the following arguments the first motivated assertion is of a personal nature and therefore rejected by the listener, whereas the second one sounds like a reasonable motivation, and puts an end to the argument. The party who offers it, however, uses content and style in a redundant way (motivated assertion + volume escalation), not realizing the weight of the assertion.

Ma: ...Yeah, gimme that gun.

Mi: Why ?

Ma: Cause I need it.

Mi: I don't wanna.

Ma: I've got it. (screaming) You didn't buy it.

(*1st PS/Mi-Ma*)

The supportive evidence in an argument about one's knowledge may appear in the form of a correct answer to a question meant to test that knowledge.

O : What goes in the zoo, Milvia ?

Ma: I know, I know better.

Mi: *I* know better.

Ma: No, *I* know better.

Mi: (holds a gun) I this an animal, Martin ?

Ma: No, that's a gun...

(*1st PS/Mi-Ma*)

Children understand the force of a motivated opinion, when this is not of a personal nature, and cease to argue. In the following argument Milvia tries hard and succeeds in providing supportive evidence for her claim to the bottle. The addressee accepts it and changes the argument into pure play; moreover, he marks the end of the argument by directing her to laugh.

(at lunch)

Mi: This is your plate. I'll get the minkie (= baby-talk for milk and drinking bottle)

Ma: (holds the bottle) There's nothing in it.

Mi: It's *my* bottle. Belongs to *me*.

Ma: There's nothing in it.

Mi: But I'm gonna nehmen mit up to my mom, so you can't take it.

Ma: I turned it over.

Mi: No, don't turn over !

Ma: (laughs) It fell down. Laugh !

(both laugh)

(*1st PS/Mi-Ma*)

The argument is a complex speech event. The children in this study are in the process of learning how to handle it. Whereas Sean avoids this type of involvement in the conversation, Milvia argues endlessly. The point-counterpoint technique, another common form of argument among children, is one of the first things she learned from her interactions with other children -- she quickly turns it into material for language play.

(in the car)

O : (to Mi) Who's your best friend in school ?

Mi: Opa (= Grandpa)

Ma: I have four opas.

Mi: I have five.

Ma: I have six.

Mi: I have seven.

Ma: I have eight.

O : Do you really have eight grandpas ?

Mi: We play.

Ma: Shut up, sil ! (to O)

(March 22, *Diary*)

From among the stylistic features of an argument, volume and speed are probably the first to be acquired. Stress is one suprasegmental element which foregrounds segments from an utterance; even if the utterance is a repetition of a previous utterance, stressing the relevant segment for the purpose of the argument presupposes good understanding of the utterance and marks the beginning of the analysis of an otherwise mechanically repeated whole. In understanding the "key" of this particular speech event, children proceed from reliance on stylistic features to content variation and eventually to motivated opinions, i.e., collaboration in abstract thought. For second language learners (and first language learners, for that matter) the attempt to offer motivated opinions is a good opportunity to use language creatively in order to suit one's purposes in an argument. To echo Piaget, "it may well be that through quarrelling children first come to feel the need for making themselves understood."

Milvia, with an acute sense of debate, does not avoid any type of conversational difficulty. Otherwise careful about mixing her two codes (German and English), she will even resort to German in order to get her opinion through. She learns the second language at a faster pace than Sean; I believe that one of the reasons for this difference is her active immersion in conversation-play.

5.3 A matter of flexibility

All through this study Sean and Milvia kept their two codes separate. Even though they share the same first language and have repeatedly been encouraged to speak to each other in German, they never did. The observer's attempts to address them in German went unheeded. Martin's attempts to introduce a German word in their conversations were considered funny jokes, as in the following example.

Mi: I want an apple.

Ma: Apfel, you say Apfel.

Mi: (laughs) No, apple, apple.

(February 15, *Diary*)

In Swain's study (1972) of bilingual children, her subjects had been exposed to both languages (English and French) since birth and acquired their "primary language" -- one code containing elements from the two languages -- from adults, before they were old enough to play with other children. Likewise, Leopold's daughter, Hildegard, constructed a unified linguistic medium of her own out of the bilingual presentation, and did not associate at first the language with definite persons.

Milvia and Sean *added* the second language when they started playing with other children. Although they are very young, and therefore it is reasonable to assume that they process the two languages by the "basic neurological system", rather than by developing "infrasystems" to deal with the second language (Lamandella 1977), their language learning process differs from that of children who are exposed to two languages from infancy.

The two children seem to use one common strategy in their use of the two languages: "German is my mother tongue, English is my peers' language." The only English formulas which "invaded" their German and took over at the expense of their German equivalents were two greeting formulas in Sean's case (*Hi* and *good-bye*) and a thanking formula in Milvia's case (*Thank you*). This happened before they could speak any English at all, and it may be due to the fact that they were so frequently spoken to the children by adult strangers. From this point on they developed different strategies in learning the second language.

In Fillmore's study all five learners acquired at first a number of formulaic expressions, which permitted them to enter the conversations with native speakers before they acquired any language rules. Subsequently, after repeated usage of these formulas in appropriate situations, the children started to analyze them and form more general rules about the way the new language functions, which eventually enabled them to use language creatively. Based on the children's assumption that "what people are saying is directly relevant to the situation at hand, or to what they or you are experiencing", an important strategy these children used was: "Get some expressions you understand, and start talking." (Fillmore 1976:639). It has been shown (Carroll 1963) that one important skill for learning a second language -- albeit in formal classroom situations -- is the ability to learn by heart a large number of utterances in a short time.

The learners in the present study came into their peers' world equipped with a number of formulas, limited enough to reduce them to silence when they started to play with other children. Aside from greeting and thanking formulas, which are not of great use in child-child conversations anyway, they knew a couple of names for familiar objects in their environment. These were learned from occasional "lessons" with English-speaking adults.

In the dynamic interaction among children one has to act promptly -- your partners do not have the patience to wait until you search your memory for an appropriate word. In such a situation Sean was satisfied with the role of an active observer. The most striking conversational strategy he seemed to use was related to his good rote memory: at a time when his knowledge of English was very limited he would surprise his interlocutor with a verbal outburst which disrupted the flow of conversation. One such verbal outburst was triggered by a relatively irrelevant utterance from his conversational partner, and was delivered, as in dramatic play, with an intonation that belonged to someone other than the actor himself. Sean's intonation pattern was mellowed down, his gestures became gentle suggesting a mother speaking to her child.

Ma: ...I'll take off my shoes just like you. (to O)

Se: Wanna sleep ? A littel whi' ? When
we wake up, when we wake up then...
Sleep a littel whi' ?

Ma: I don't. What wire ? (angry)

Se: I say (angry) (then in sing-song
voice) Wanna sleep a littel whi' ?

(*2nd PS/Se-Ma*)

Most likely Sean had a rather large number of such rehearsed speech samples in his repertoire tha t he used in the play-sessions. Like an adult who likes to drop Latin adages in the flow of a conversation, Sean had to be observant and wait for the right moment; but this moment may never arise during an intimate verbal interaction.

In another conversational episode -- "Why doesn't the lion talk ?" -- Sean, active at first, seems to lose interest in the topic only to come with a surprising answer -- "Why, he's shy." The difficulty of the utterance is twofold: first, the semantics of the connector "why" is rather complex in that it signifies that the answer to the question is a unique and obvious one, as opposed to a possible answer among many; second, the peculiar intonation (Fall-Rise-Fall) is hard to reproduce by a non-native speaker, and even more so by a child who has barely any English at all. As to the appropriate use of the connector, it seems that for Sean it is rehearsed speech, heard when the question was asked of himself -- "Why doesn't he talk ?". However, what was obvious in the speech situation in which the utterance was first heard -- a child does not talk because he is shy -- may not be equally appropriate when the question is asked about an animal.

Dore (1973) showed that infants learning a first language approach the task differently, which may be a direct consequence of their mothers' approach to mother-child interaction. The more "didactic" mothers, that is, those mothers who teach their children endlessly naming objects, would most likely shape "word-babies", children who heavily rely on their knowledge of correct words in order to carry on a conversation. These children would inevitably be slower talkers, for it takes longer to acquire the correct froms than to be expressive with few words, which is what "prosodic-babies" do. The mothers of such babies behave more or less as a child conversational partner would do: for them language is a means to communicate and not a subject-matter to be taught. Their children will approach language learning through intonation and gradually fill in the intonation contours with correct forms as their language develops.

To what extent can this rather simplifying distinction be applied to second language learners ? Do children use the same strategy in second language learning as they did in learning their first language ? Does the kind of verbal input they receive -- if the input provider is different in the second language learning situation -- determine the strategies they adopt ? The answers to these questions will evidently hold true only in the case of the two subjects involved in the present study. Moreover, the answers are based on observation rather than on "objective" measurements.

No data are available about Sean's first 18 months. At about that age his comprehension of German was resonably good for a child his age, while his production was rather telegraphic. He was not what is commonly called a "verbal child". He was not eager to talk with anyone, including his caretakers; this made his caretakers confused about his ability to understand: they would check on his comprehension by naming objects and requesting him to point to them, a rather formal classroom-like situation at a very early age. This apparently raised his frustration threshold to a point where he would refuse to play the pointing game; evidence of this was later obtained when Sean refused to play the same pointing game with the observer on the Peabody Picture Vocabulary Test.

In his conversations with Martin, Sean often showed concern with correct forms and anger if he thought his partner did not understand him, as in the following examples:

Ma: People swim. Do you go swimming everyday with this ?

Se: Yeah. In water, in a water...(louder) *I said* in the water.

(*3rd PS/Se-Ma*)

Ma: Here's another frog, in the pond.

Se: It's poidonous. (louder) It's poi-do-nous.

(*3rd PS/Se-Ma*)

Se: Dez no drivers in dere. 's break...bro... *broken.*

(*3rd PS/Se-Ma*)

Even though his conversational partner seldom teased him about his pronunciation, he would often correct himself and simultaneously get angry at his playmate. It appears that this kind of frustration comes from his first language learning experience, although the input provider is different in the second language situation. Sean does not talk unless he knows what to say and how to say it correctly. He prefers to observe. Sean seems to be a "word-baby". The conversations with Sean are structured very slowly: the search for referents can go on for ever, without any attempt on Sean's part to establish a conversation in play.

Milvia is not a cautious child. She eagerly plunges into the unknown, argues to exhaustion, may even resort to her first language if the situation requires a very prompt response she cannot promptly produce out of her second language repertoire. She never confines herself to the role of an observer; she is an active participant even when the meaning of the situation is not very clear to her.

(on the slide in the park)

Ma: I'm the road runner.

Mi: I'm the brunner too.

(August 18, *Diary*)

She is eager to establish an intimate style with her conversational partner, which means picking up his pet phrases and using them when the situation seems appropriate.

(They meet early in the morning: Milvia is wearing a dress, Martin is wearing overalls; usually they both wear overalls and Martin remarks each time "We are both dressed the same.")

Mi: Hey, we are both dressed the same.

Ma: No, no, no, Milvia. You have a dress and I have my Osh-Kosh.

Mi: Both the same.

Ma: Each is different.

Mi: Both, both, both...you said so.

Ma: I said each.

Mi: O.K., O.K., each, but you said so.

(July 23, *Diary*)

Milvia often initiates "pretend" conversations or deftly modifies the topics initiated by her conversational partner; their conversation-play does not require much structuring before it takes off. Her main aim is to establish a conversation-play in which her status is equal to that of her partner. The second language emerges quite effortlessly out of such interactions. She corrects herself only if her partner requests correction and only if she feels that her failure to self-correct would result in a breakdown in communication. For her communication is no less enjoyable because she lacks linguistic fluency. In an entirely enpressured situation, as conversation-play between children is, if there is a will to communicate, one has always several ways at his disposal. Milvia's flexible approach to conversation ensures successful and effortless second language learning; she may be said to be a "prosodic-baby".

5.4 A matter of ambiguity

In the case of the two learners in the present study, who started learning the second language not young enough to be completely unconscious about the peculiar situation they were faced with, the new language situation may seem extremely ambiguous, the first major ambiguous situation in their life. The different degrees of tolerance to ambiguity they possess may therefore play a significant role in the ease with which they learn the second language, the ease with which they switch the two codes, in the maintenance of the two languages.

Psychologists suggest that children with intolerance to ambiguity find different strategies to reduce ambiguity-induced anxiety, such as avoidance of complex situations, limitation of one's attention on few elements in a complex situation, or premature structuring of a complex situation (Harrington, Block, and Block 1977). Faced with new and unmastered situations, some individuals react in resourceful and flecible ways -- they are said to be adaptive personalities, characterized among other things by a high degree of tolerance to ambiguity. Other individuals react in the same circumstances in rigid, inflexible ways, unable to cope effectively with a complex, dynamic situation -- they are said to be characterized among other things by intolerance to ambiguity.

Any situation which cannot be handled with old, available methods can be said to be ambiguous. Second language learning in any circumstances is ambiguous: an individual who knows how to communicate in a language is suddenly faced with a new communicative situation which requires the knowledge of another language in order for any communication to occur at all.

The learners in the present study are actually faced with two ambiguous situations simultaneously: one is the new type of social situations, conversation-play with one's age-peers, a new style of communication, whose rules have to be sorted out; the other is the second language, which is the prerequisite for the realization of the first situation. When both new situations occur at the same time, it is reasonable to assume that the strategy developed for handling one situation will be reflected in the way the other situation is dealt with. In our case, the strategies the two children develop for handling the task of second language learning will be reflected in the strategies developed for coping with the new social situation.

Samples of the children's conversation-play provide evidence of the way they approach the new social situation and language learning to the extent to which it is essential in handling the social situation. The two learners are different in the way they approach the two tasks. The end result is also different, in that one child knows more English by the end of the study and is a more efficient conversational partner than the other. Therefore, their strategies in handling the task of second language learning, as reflected in their strategies for coping with the new social situation, seem to account for their success or failure in achieving both tasks.

From observation alone we have seen that the more successful of the two learners, Milvia, does not remove herself from any situation --

verbal or non-verbal -- and argues endlessly with her partner, but also knows when to give in, is tenacious, but also resourceful and flexible; in a word, she seems to respond effectively to the requirements of the dynamic situation. The other learner, Sean, avoids involvement when it requires non-habitual responses, prefers to observe until the situation evokes a familiar situational context, requires more structuring of the social situation.

In order to communicate Milvia puts to use all her resources (first code, intonation, imitation). For her it is more important not to give up her part of an active conversational partner than to be perfectly accurate in her use of the second code. Sean, on the other hand, retreats into his shell when the situation is unfamiliar and cannot be handled with available means.

After six months of observation the two learners were presented with two experimental situations: a) the Lowenfeld Mosaic Test (1954), considered to be a highly ambiguous unstructured task for young children; b) a comprehension task based on Dunn's Peabody Picture Vocabulary Test (1959), a structured task, which could still be considered ambiguous because it requires code-switching.

The *Lowenfeld Mosaic Test* was individually administered by the observer in the presence of the child's mother. The observer had promised the children that she would play a new game with them, and they were both looking forward to the occasion.

The test consists of 229 plastic chips of different colors and geometric shapes (48 diamonds, 24 squares, 72 scalenes, 49 isosceles triangles, 36 equilateral triangles, arranged in a box according to shape) and a rectangular wooden tray covered with white paper. The children were shown the plastic chips, they named the colors together with the observer, and were finally told to play with them: "You can play with the pieces on the tray; use as many as you want, do whatever you want with them." It should be pointed out that both children were familiar with this kind of game: Milvia had a commercial game of the same type with magnetic plastic chips; Sean frequently played a non-figurative game with larger wooden pieces at school.

Several factors were measured: the time between the instruction and the beginning of the work, the working time, the number of pieces used, the shapes and colors used. When the children finished the design they were asked if they wanted to play any longer and, if the response was negative, the observer took a photograph of the child's production.

Milvia started to work right away. She used 15 pieces (7 white, 3 green, 2 yellow, 2 red, and 1 blue) and four shapes; she placed triangles back to back twice and squares once; otherwise the pieces were spread all over the tray, and no particular shape emerged when the design was completed. She finished the design in thirty seconds, announced the observer that she had finished it, and remarked "I like white pieces", smiling her teasing smile. Half an hour later she asked the observer to give the game back to her and said:" This time I'm gonna use all the pieces." She kept her promise, emptied the box on the table, took two handful of chips and dumped them on the tray.

Sean did not touch the pieces for 40 minutes after the instruction. During this time he repeatedly complained about the difficulty of the task, and asked his mother to show him how to do it. His mother made a geometric floral design in the center of the tray using only triangles of different colors. Then the pieces were removed from the tray, and Sean was asked to do something with them himself. He complained again about the difficulty of the task. He was left alone with the mosaic in his room. His father also helped him by making a floral design in the middle of the tray using only triangular shapes. After 40 minutes and two demonstrations Sean made a design on one side of the tray using eight squares (2 blue, 1 green, one red, and 3 white), and called the observer to look at it.

Given the informal character of the "testing", the most important aspect of the results seems to be their "history", i.e., the way the final design was arrived at, rather than the computerization of shapes and colors for the assessment of imagination, premature structuring, and so on. The history of the results is unobtainable in a large scale experiment, but then in a true experiment a subject like Sean would have been eliminated -- no one is allowed to demonstrate to the child what he is supposed to do with the plastic pieces. For the purpose of this study, the *approach* in dealing with an ambiguous situation of a non-verbal type seems more important than the end result.

Sean avoided the new -- albeit not entirely unfamiliar -- situation. Had he produced his final design without any help, his approach would have been labeled "tendency to impose premature structure on an unstructured situation". As things are, it is quite obvious that he required more structure, but he appealed to an adult figure to impose the structure he needed; the end result is a mere replication of an adult solution.

Milvia approached the situation without much concern about the form or the content of her response. She did the task in order to satisfy her curiosity. Not only was she not eager to please the observer, but her final remark shows that she was ready to fight for her solution: she used mostly white chips because she *chose* to do so.

If one looks back at the way in which the learners behave (verbally and non-verbally) in their conversation-play with Martin, the results to this test could have been easily predicted. Had the results not been consistent with the observed spontaneous behavior of the children, one could have concluded that either the test did not measure what it was supposed to measure or that nonverbal ambiguity is quite different from verbal ambiguity. As things stand with the two learners in the present study, one is tempted to think that the two types of ambiguity are not qualitatively different.

In order to assess their comprehension of English and German, the learners were asked to respond to the observer's utterance in English by pointing to one of the four pictures on the page of a *Peabody Picture Vocabulary Test*. ("Look at the four pictures and point to the one I tell you to.") The task was repeated in German with the mothers describing the picture. The two children were tested on pages 15 to 40 from the test.

Sean refused to play the pointing game with the observer. He did the German part with his mother, and responded correctly to 24 out of 26 items, that is, over 90% of the items. He asked to do the English part also with his mother, but after four items he started laughing and pointing to the wrong picture. He kept asking questions in German about pictures described to him in English and refused to continue the game.

Milvia accepted the task with one modification: rather than pointing she requested that she color the picture. In English she responded correctly to 16 out of 26 items, that is, to a little over 60% of the items. In German she responded correctly to 21 items, that is, in 80% of the cases. She was more interested in pictures representing actions, on which she would comment, as in the following example.

O : The boy is having a haircut.

Mi: Why is the man cutting his hair ?

Started as a measure of comprehension, the results of the task seem less interesting than the approach the children took in handling it. (The results point to Sean's slightly higher ability in comprehending German words.)

Once again Sean appealed to parental guidance for handling the task. The non-habitual situation of having his mother speak English to him destroys his equilibrium: he does not continue the task, refusing to switch to another code, even if only receptively.

Milvia gets involved in the game right away, provided some of the rules are modified so as to suit her. She shows a pronounced preference for action pictures, which points again to the fact that for her language is mainly used to regulate social interactions with others.

In her study of vocabulary development in very young children Katherine Nelson (1973) suggests that children differ in the types of words they learn first, along a continuum between *referential children*, i.e., children mostly concerned with objects and their properties, and *expressive children*, i.e., children concerned with establishing relationships with other people. Along this continuum Sean seems to fall closer to the referential extreme, whereas Milvia consistently shows an interest in regulating her social interaction with other people.

Receptive code switching is unquestionably much less problematic than productive code switching. However, if code switching is an ambiguous situation, as I believe it is, then the relative ease with which one switches codes can signal degrees of tolerance to ambiguity. Whereas Sean seems puzzled by the unusual juxtaposition of the two codes in the Peabody Picture Vocabulary Test situation, Milvia does not question the situation at all. Furthermore, by the end of the study Milvia productively switched the two codes with maximum ease, while Sean reportedly ceased to use his first language productively at the age of 3;3.

5.5 Summary

Children who learn a second language from other children, in interactions with their age-peers, vary in the way in which they approach the language learning task.

Part of this variation is due to the "conversational style" children bring to the task from their first language learning experience. Thus, from a very early age children can be said to have a "conversational style", in much the same way in which they have a personality, a temperament, etc. At one extreme of the conversational style continuum we have individuals who show more interest in regulating social interactions with others than in being correct and clear; they are verbally quick, expressive to the point of being aggressive, ready to get involved in verbal fights, but also eager to reach a truce provided they are to be treated as equals by their conversational partners. At the other extreme we have those who think before they leap into a verbal interaction; they seem to be more interested in correctness and processibility, they are reluctant to attack conversational difficulties and perfectly at ease when the conversation is lagging.

Neither conversational style is more commendable than the other, as few extremes are. How many times did we wish we had kept quiet, but also how many times did we wish we had said more and reduced our conversational partner to silence !

Likewise, neither conversational style alone makes a better second language learner. However, it may well be the case that each conversational style would feel more comfortable in a different second language learning situation; what may be a stifling speech situation for one style may well prove to be optimal for another.

The other part of the variation is due to task specific factors. Second language learning is an ambiguous task, particularly at such an early age, when one cannot yet properly speak of motivation, attitudes towards the speakers of the other language, social distance, etc. The children in the present study may have encountered other ambiguous situations before their exposure to the second language. Second language learning represents a rather complex ambiguous situation: Why does one have to learn a first language when as soon as one goes into the larger world that language is of no use ? How much language does one have to know in order to interact with one's age-peers ? Is there any use in maintaining the first language ? Why do some people speak two language when the majority do not ?

Again, at one end of the continuum of approaches to an ambiguous situation we have individuals who accept the situation as such and look for help in the environment in order to effectively cope with it, while at the other end we have individuals who question the new situation and feel lost in it.

In the second language situation we are dealing with, the ambiguity is existential rather than linguistic. The approach to such an existentially ambiguous situation may not necessarily help or hinder the acquisition of the second language per se, but it may accelerate or slow down the process of acquisition. More importantly, it can have an effect on later developments, such as first language maintenance and the ease in code switching, which characterize bilingual individuals.

6. CONCLUSIONS

6.1 General findings

The present study followed two German-speaking children for six months, from the moment they started playing with other children, in an attempt to show how children start socializing with other children of the same age without knowledge of the societal language and how they start learning the societal language in order to successfully socialize with their age-peers.

My goal was to investigate the second language acquisition process of two young children who were first exposed to the second language in interactions with their age-peers. More specifically, the present study aimed at showing the relationship between the pace at which a second language is acquired, as well as the relative effort required by the task, and the conversational style the child brings to the task of second language learning.

The data on which the study was based consisted of naturally occurring conversations between two learners of English and one English-speaking child, as well as two informally administered tests, one for measuring the comprehension of the two languages by the learners and another one for measuring the learners' tolerance of ambiguity.

Learning a second language in early childhood is thought to be an effortless process, free of frustrations and anxieties, since it takes place in an unpressured, non-competitive atmosphere. However, learning a second language when you already have a reasonably good means of communication through your first language may be to the child a rather puzzling situation, much more so than an adult, who is aware of the great number sociocultural factors at play in the world.

Children who are born in a linguistic environment other than the one of the larger community in which they live are faced with this puzzling situation when they start socializing outside the family.[3] They come into the new sociolinguistic situation as willing communicators, eager to be absorbed into the world of their peers. They also bring into this new world their own "conversational styles", the result of their interactions with adult caretakers. Their styles are reflected in their conversational strategies, in the ways they approach conversation-play with other children. It was shown that learning a second language in the speech situation characterized as conversation-play with one's peers is directly related to the conversational styles children bring to the task, that is, that contrary to the widespread opinion that "children have everything going for them" in learning a second language, individual differences in learning a second language are as pronounced with very young children as they are with adults.

Conversation-play among children is a speech situation characterized by quickness and expressiveness. In order to be quick and expressive one does not necessarily have to have a fully developed linguistic code at his disposal; children are conversationally fluent long before they have fully acquired their native tongue. Conversational style does not seem to be exactly a matter of choice, however; one's "style" seems to be beyond one's control very early in life. How much of it shaped by the environment and how much was there to begin with is still an open question. Suffice it to say here that, as far as second language is concerned, whether you "pick it up in the street" or you learn it "methodically" in the classroom, young children, as well as older children and adults, differ immensely in terms of the effort they put into it and the pace at which they learn it. What seems to distinguish children from adults is not so much the nature of the process as the end result: whereas there is no knowledge of normal young children who do not eventually master the language of the environment they live in, adults who achieve native-like mastery of the second language seem to be the exception rather than the rule.

The main finding of this study has to do with individual differences in learning a second language at a very early age, when children without older children begin socializing with other children in the societal language. If indeed individual differences in first language acquisition are of a trivial nature, in that no serious consequences can be attributed to them, one cannot claim the same thing about individual differences in second language acquisition. It was speculated before that by the time they are of school age the learners in this study will be linguistically undistinguishable from native speakers of English. At this point, however, this claim cannot be made with absolute certainty. Even if this were the case, there remains a second problem: bilingualism.

A number of studies (e.g., Child 1943; Peal and Lambert 1962; Gardner and Lambert 1972) point out that linguistic and cultural "renounciation" (as well as "segregation") does not have a beneficial effect on the psychological identity of the potential bilingual. It was shown in the present study that a certain approach to language learning favors renounciation of the first language. This becomes a serious problem when one takes into account the fact that potential bilinguals are not isolated cases, but rather large populations of children for whose balanced development we are responsible.

The second finding of this study has to do with measurement of language development in young children. In the whole study no mention was made of the MLU of the two learners as indices of linguistic maturity. This is not surprising in a model based on dynamic interaction. A major drawback of this frequently used measure of linguistic maturity became apparent at the very beginning of the study. In order to compute Milvia's MLU on the first twenty utterances in the first recorded conversation the investigator did not have to go beyond the first page of the transcript, whereas in order to compute the same measure on Sean's utterances one had to pick up twenty utterances from at least three pages of typed conversation. (An utterance is taken to be one major tone unit; thus, one conversational turn may contain several utterances.) The MLU did not significantly differ with the two learners, either at the beginning of the study (MLU_{Mi} = 2.73; MLU_{Se} = 2.40) or after six months of interaction in the second language (MLU_{Mi} = 3.10; MLU_{Se} = 2.74). A striking difference was found in *conversational density*, i.e., the ratio between the number of utterances produced by the learner and the number of utterances produced by his conversational partner across a set stretch of discourse. According to this measure, the two learners differed significantly: in Milvia's case the ratio is 1:1, whereas in Sean's case it is 1:2, across twenty conversational turns.

Conversational density reveals the degree of verbal involvement in a conversation. In itself it is not necessarily a measure of linguistic maturity, but in combination with the MLU it can show how much (or how little) can be achieved conversationally with very little language. In the present study the two learners with comparable MLU's differ in the way they make use of their linguistic knowledge in the dynamics of interaction.

The third finding of this study is related to the problem of "testing" very young children. Anyone who has done research with young children knows how unpredictable their response to a structured task can be. With older subjects, lack of cooperation leads to their elimination from the investigated sample of the population. With young subjects the common conclusion is that they cannot perform reasonably on a certain task and, as long as they are not able to perform, their competence is held in doubt.

However, as observers of young children know and as the present study tried to show, young children do get involved -- to different extents -- in highly structured conversations and games and, when the situation is unstructured, work hard at providing it with a structure of sorts. Faced with a task whose structure is imposed by an experimenter, children behave as differently as they do in naturally occurring conversations: some show resistance and inflexibility, others negotiate the situation with the experimenter, still others perform in a perfunctory way to please the experimenter.

What this study seems to suggest is that, with very young children, the way they approach non-verbal tasks designed for them may be at least equally important as the actual "results" on the test: it may reveal the way in which children approach verbal tasks and, consequently, the way in which they acquire language. In other words, children seem to behave consistently across tasks, so that behavior on one type of task can predict behavior on a different type of task. We can thus speak about children having a consistent "method of discovery".

The present study also suggests a number of implications for further research and educational practice.

6.2 Implications for research

The present study tries to fill a gap in second language acquisition research, a gap that had appeared between studies of infants who are exposed to two languages from birth and who receive language input from adult caretakers and older children who add a second language but also receive language input primarily form adults on the one hand, and studies of school-aged children who receive language input both in the classroom and from their age-peers outside school, on the other hand. The first category of studies did not concern themselves with individual differences between learners, because they either chose to study one subject alone or, when they studied several children, they chose to focus on commonalities in language acquisition rather than on differences. In the second category of studies the differences between learners of a second language were too striking to be ignored. The present study, investigating naturally occurring conversations between children, when they first socialize with other children in the societal language, could not fail to record the differences in the way very young children approach the task of second language learning.

An ever larger number of studies seem to point in the same direction: children exhibit tremendous differences in second language learning when they add the new language at the earliest possible age (after the age of two); differences exist to an unmistakable degree when children add a second language around school age; differences are very pronounced after puberty; furthermore, differences are observed in first language acquisition. One needs to take a fresh look at children learning two languages simultaneously from birth with a new emphasis: on differences rather than on similarities. But, most importantly, a model for language learning (first or second) has to be formulated which could account for all these differences.

If indeed it is shown that people perform differently with respect to language learning irrespective of age, number of languages, and type of linguistic input, the following question arises: what makes them perform differently ? Are children born with different "methods of discovery" ? Are these "methods of discovery" the same across tasks, verbal and non-verbal ?

The present study suggests that, at least at the age with which the study is concerned, children do perform consistently across tasks, at least some tasks. The "methods of discovery" have to do with what is called "cognitive styles" and "personality factors" (Fillmore 1978; Strong and Cathcart 1978). The present study does not investigate the cognitive or personality styles of the learners for the simple reason that there is no appropriate way of measuring such parameters on very young children. However, there is no reason to believe that measures of style in very young children cannot be devised such as to *predict* children's approach to language learning rather than *confirm* their observed behavior, as was the case in the present study.

Finally, this study suggests that different approaches to language learning, as reflected in conversational style, affect the pace at which the language is learned. It was shown that active language use (as measured by "conversational density") leads to faster language learning; involvement in verbal interaction, rather than avoidance and concern with correct grammatical forms, seems to characterize a good second language learner. A further direction of research would consist of investigating to what extent this is true of older children and adults, or what combinations of strategies make a good language learner at different ages.

During the investigation of the children's conversations several aspects of child-child interaction were pointed out which seem to belong to language learning in general, rather than to second language acquisition as a specific language learning situation.

One such aspect is the way children develop means of organizing a conversation, which seem to differ from adults' conversational architecture. The conversational organizers children develop (e.g., the attention children pay to identification of referents in the economy of a conversation) explain the high frequency of certain utterances in child language; such utterances are usually referred to as "routines". A closer analysis of routines in child language with an emphasis on their role in conversation, as well as the types of verbal routines children use in their conversations with adults as opposed to their age-peers, would certainly enrich the picture of child language acquisition.

6.3 Implications for education

In recent years the problem of individual differences in learning has become a real concern for educators. Monolingual children can benefit from self-paced programs, based on the awareness that children differ in the way they approach different types of tasks and in terms of the pace at which they pick up new skills, language-related or not.

The educational policy for bilingual or potentially bilingual children -- albeit controversial and differently implemented -- takes into consideration one dimension along which these children differ, that is, the knowledge of the societal language when they come to school. Thus, linguistically different children fall into one of the three categories: children who have good, little, or no knowledge of the societal language. The last two categories can benefit from bilingual education. Even though bilingual education exists in a multitude of forms, basically the second language is *taught* in the classroom and expressive use is made of syntactic-pattern drills. Whether the classroom has a number of native speakers of the societal language or not, the main input provider is the teacher. More often than not, the socialization outside school takes place in the children's first language. In the classroom little or no attention is paid to the different ways in which children approach the task of second language learning.

As this study tried to show, some children feel comfortable imitating adult speech, while others do not. There is little room for the verbally agressive child in the classroom, where docility and conformity are the most highly rewarded attributes. Such a child needs more than drills with syntactic patterns; if the process of language learning is to be facilitated for him, he needs plenty of opportunities for spontaneity in interaction. Such opportunities are abundant in child-child interaction, that is, in interactions with native speakers of the target language from the same age group as the learner; such interactions can take place not only in the school-yard, but also in the classroom, under direct supervision by the teacher. The teacher, as planner and coordinator of child-child "happenings" in the classroom, will thus have access to a great deal more than correct acquisition of morphemes by the learners, namely, to the appropriate use of language by the learners in the dynamic interaction with their age-peers. The teacher may well be surprised to notice that the good pattern producers and imitators are not always equally skillful at manipulating language spontaneously. The teacher will thus be able to obtain a much richer profile of the language learner.

As far as the other side of the coin is concerned -- the maintenance and development of the native language by the learners -- it is again in the process of naturally occurring interactions among children that a good observer will detect the first signs of first language renounciation, which, more often than not, are accompanied by another phenomenon: the native speakers of the societal language do not acquire the language of their peers. If it is the common aim of both parents and teachers to develop true bilinguals out of potentially bilingual children, then the instruction in one language has to match the instruction in the other language, for in a truly bilingual program one cannot speak about one target language, but rather about two sets of targets: the acquisition and development of the societal language and the development of the native language for one group of children, and the acquisition and development of a second language and the development of the societal language for the other group of children. Obviously, the bilingual teacher is faced with a much more complex situation than any other educator, but then so are the children whose cooperation he needs and ought to take more advantage of.

FOOTNOTES

1. I would like to express my gratitude to Lily Fillmore, Charles Fillmore, Herb Simons and Ruth Cathcart for their friendship, guidance and encouragement during the writing of this study.

2. The technique of insisting that a certain child answer the question after it has been answered correctly and spontaneously by another child may easily be interpreted as indirect disagreement with the initial answer and direction to search for another answer. However, it seems unlikely that this is the case here: Milvia likes to tease and make her partner angry; she smiles as she is giving the wrong answer, taking the observer into her confidence.

3. The situation may be different when there are older siblings in the family.

REFERENCES

Bloom, Lois
1970 Language development: Form and function in emerging grammars. Cambridge, Mass.: MIT Press.

Brenneis, D. and L. Lein
1977 "'You Fruithead': A sociolinguistic approach to children's dispute". In S. Ervin -Tripp and C. Mitchell-Kernan (eds.), Child discourse. New York: Academic Press.

Bruner, Jerome S.
1972 "Nature and uses of immaturity". American Psychologist 8:27. 687-708.

Bruner, Jerome S.
1975 "The ontogenesis of speech acts". Journal of Child Language 2:1.1-19.

Carroll, John B.
1963 "Research on teaching foreign languages". In N.L. Gage (ed.), Handbook of research in teaching. Chicago: Rand McNally.

Child, I.L.
1943 Italian or American ? The second generation in conflict. New Haven: Yale University Press.

Chomsky, Noam
1965 Aspects of the theory of syntax. Cambridge, Mass.: MIT Press.

Clark, Eve V.
1973 "How children describe time and order". In C.A. Ferguson and D.I. Slobin (eds.), Studies in childhood language and development. New York: Holt, Rinehart and Winston.

Clark, Eve V.
1971 "On the acquisition of the meaning of 'before' and 'after'". Journal of Verbal Learning and Verbal Behavior 10.266-275.

Cook-Gumperz, J.
1972 "The child as practical reasoner". In M. Sanchez and B. Blount (eds.), Socio-cultural dimensions of language use. New York: Academic Press.

Cook-Gumperz, J. and John J. Gumperz
1976 Context in children's speech. (= Working Paper 46.) Berkeley: Language Behavior Research Laboratory.

Dolan, Carolyn L.
1972 "A method for film analysis of ethnic communication style", Paper presented at the Annual Meeting of the Society for Applied Anthropology, Montreal, Quebec.

Dore, John
1973 The development of speech acts. Unpublished doctoral dissertation. New York: City University of New York.

Dore, John
1977 "'On them sheriff': A pragmatic analysis of children's response to questions". In S. Ervin-Tripp and C. Mitchell-Kernan (eds.), Child discourse. New York: Academic Press.

Dulay, H. and M. Burt
1974 "Natural sequences in child second language acquisition". Working Papers in Bilingualism 3.45-66.

Dunn, L.M.
1959 Peabody picture vocabulary test. Circle Pines, Minn.: American Guidance Service, Inc.

Erickson, Frederick
1973 Final report of project #MH 18230, MH 21460, "Inter-ethnic relations in urban institutional settings" (with J. Shultz, C. Dolan, D. Pariser, M. Erder).

Erickson, Frederick and J. Shultz
n.d. "'When is a context ?': Some issues and methods in the analysis of social competence". Ms.

Ervin-Tripp, Susan M.
1964 "Imitation and structural change in children's language". In Michel Lane (ed.), Introduction to structuralism. New York: Basic Books.

Ervin-Tripp, Susan M.
1967 "An Issei learns English". Journal of Social Issues 23:2.78-90.

Ervin-Tripp, Susan M.
1977 "Wait for me rollerskate !". In S.M. Ervin-Tripp and C. Mitchell-Kernan (eds.), Child Discourse. New York: Academic Press.

Ervin-Tripp, Susan M.
1978 "Children's verbal turn-taking". Ms.

Evans, R.I.
1973 Jean Piaget: The man and his ideas. New York: Dutton.

Fillmore, Lily W.
1976 The second time around: Cognitive and social strategies in second language acquisition. Unpublished doctoral dissertation.

Stanford University.

Fillmore, Lily W.
1978 "Sources of individual variation in second language acquisition". Paper presented at the Los Angeles Second Language Research Forum, October 6-8.

Flavell, John H.
1966 "La langue privé". Bulletin de Psychologie 19.698-701.

Fraser, C., R. Brown, and U. Bellugi
1963 "Control of grammar in imitation, comprehension, and production". Journal of Verbal Learning and Verbal Behavior 2.121-135.

Gardner, R.C. and W.E. Lambert
1972 Attitudes and motivation in second language acquisition. Rowley, Mass.: Newbury House.

Garvey, Catherine
1975 "Requests and responses in children's speech". Journal of Child Language 2.41-62.

Garvey, Catherine
1977 "Play with language and speech". In S. Ervin-Tripp and C. Mitchell-Kernan (eds.), Child discourse. New York: Academic Press.

Garvey, C. and R. Hogan
1973 "Social speech and social interaction: Egocentrism revisited". Child Development 44.562-568.

Gough, J.W.
1975 Comparative studies in second language learning. CAL-ERIC CLL Series on Language and Linguistics 26. Washington D.C.: Center for Applied Linguistics.

Hakuta, K.
1974 "Report on the development of grammatical morphemes in a Japanese girl learning English as a second language". Working Papers in Bilingualism 3.19-43.

Halliday, M.A.K. and R. Hasan
1976 Cohesion in English. London: Longman.

Harrington, D.M., J.H. Block, and J. Block
1977 "Intolerance of ambiguity in preschool children: Psychometric considerations, behavioral manifestations, and parental correlates". Ms.

Hatch, Evelyn
1978 "Discourse analysis and second language acquisition". In E. Hatch (ed.), Studies in second language acquisition. Rowley, Mass.: Newbury House.

Holzman, M.
1972 "The use of interrogative forms in the verbal interaction of

three mothers and their children". Journal of Psychological Research 1:4.311-336.

Hymes, Dell
1972 "Introduction: Towards ethnographies of communication". In J.J. Gumperz and D. Hymes (eds.), Directions in sociolinguistics: The ethnography of communication. New York: Holt, Rinehart, and Winston.

Hymes, Dell
1974 Foundations in sociolinguistics. Philadelphia: University of Pennsylvania Press.

Iwamura, S.
1977 "Games and other routines in the conversations of young children: A case study in developmental sociolinguistics". Ms.

Keenan, E.O.
1974 "Conversational competence in children". Journal of Child Language 1:2.163-183.

Keenan, E.O. and K. Klein
1975 "Coherence in children's discourse". Journal of Psycholinguistic Research 4:4.365-380.

Keenan, E.O. and B. Schieffelin
1975 "Topic as a discourse notion: A study of topic in the conversation of children and adults". In Charles Li (ed.), Subject and topic. New York: Academic Press.

Lamandella, J.J.
1977 "Primary and secondary language acquisition vs. foreign language learning: A neuropsychological perspective". Paper presented at the Los Angeles Second Language Research Forum.

Leopold, W.F.
1939-1949 Speech development of a bilingual child: A linguist's Record, 4 vols. Evanston, Ill.: Northwestern University Press (1939, 1947, 1949a, 1949b).

Lieven, E.
1977 "Turn-taking and pragmatics: Two issues in early child language". In R. Campbell and P.T. Smith (eds.), The Stirling psychology of language conference. New York: Plenum.

Lowenfeld, M.
1954 The Lowenfeld mosaic test. London: Newman Neame, Ltd.

McTear, Michael
1977 "How pre-school children initiate conversational exchanges". Ms.

Mehan, Hugh and H. Wood
1975 The reality of ethnomethodology. New York: John Wiley and Sons.

Mitchell-Kernan, C. and K. Kernan
1977 "Pragmatics of directive choice among children". In S. Ervin-Tripp and C. Mitchell-Kernan (eds.), Child Discourse. New York: Academic Press.

Nelson, Katherine
1973 "Structure and strategy in learning to talk". Monogr. Soc. Res. Child Dev. 38:149.

Peck, Sabrina
1977 Play in child second language acquisition. Unpublished M.A. thesis. University of California Los Angeles.

Peal, E. and W.E. Lambert
1962 "The relation of bilingualism to intelligence". Psychological Monographs 76:546.

Piaget, Jean
1926 Language and thought of the child. New American Library (1974).

Piaget, Jean
1967 Six psychological studies. New York: Vintage Books.

Piaget, Jean
1971 Les explications causales. Paris: Presses Universitaires de France.

Richards, Martin P.M.
1974 The integration of the child into a social world. Cambridge: Cambridge University Press.

Ryan, Joanna
1974 "Early language development: Towards a communicational analysis". In Martin P.M. Richards (ed.), The integration of the child into a social world. Cambridge: Cambridge University Press.

Sachs, J. and M. Johnson
1972 Language development in a hearing child of deaf parents. Report 2. Storrs, Conn.: Language Acquisition Lab, University of Connecticut.

Sacks, Harvey, E.A. Schegloff, and G. Jefferson
1974 "A simplest systematic for the organization of turn-taking in conversation". Language 50.696-735.

Schegloff, E.A. and H. Sacks
1973 "Opening up closings". Semiotica 8.289-327.

Schegloff, E.A.
1968 "Sequencing in conversational openings". American Anthropologist 70.1075-1095.

Schumann, John
1975 Second language acquisition: The pidginization hypothesis. Unpublished doctoral dissertation, Harvard University.

Scollon, Ronald T.
1974 One child's language from one or two: The origins of construction. Doctoral dissertation, University of Hawaii.

Sinclair, John and R.M. Coulthard
1975 Towards an analysis of discourse: The English used by teachers and pupils. London and New York: Oxford University Press.

Slobin, D.I.
1971 "Suggested universals in the ontogenesis of grammar". In G.B. Flores D'Arcais and J.W. Levelt (eds.), Advances in psycholinguistics. Amsterdam: North Holland.

Slobin, D.I.
1975 "Pidgin and child language". Ms.

Stalnaker, Robert
1972 "Pragmatics". In D. Davidson and G. Harman (eds.), Semantics of natural language. Dordrecht: Reidel.

Strong, Michael and Ruth Cathcart
1978 "Cognitive styles, personality, and second language acquisition in young children: Methodological issues". Paper presented at the Second Research Forum, Los Angeles, California.

Swain, M.K.
1972 Bilingualism as a first language. Unpublished doctoral dissertation, University of California Irvine.

Vygotsky, Lev
1962 Thought and language. Cambridge, Mass.: MIT Press.

In the *PRAGMATICS & BEYOND* series the following monographs have been published thus far:

1. *Anca M. Nemoianu:* The Boat's Gonna Leave: A Study of Children Learning a Second Language from Conversations with Other Children. Amsterdam, 1980. vi, 116 pp. Paperbound.

2. *Michael D. Fortescue:* A Discourse Production Model for 'Twenty Questions'. Amsterdam, 1980. x, 137 pp. Paperbound.

3. *Melvin Joseph Adler:* A Pragmatic Logic for Commands. Amsterdam, 1980. viii, 131 pp. Paperbound.

4. *Jef Verschueren:* On Speech Act Verbs. Amsterdam, 1980. viii, 83 pp. Paperbound.

Forthcoming (to be published autumn 1980):

Benoît de Cornulier: Meaning Detachment.

Marcelo Dascal: Pragmatics and the Philosophy of Mind.

Geoffrey N. Leech: Explorations in Semantics and Pragmatics.

Herman Parret: Contexts of Understanding.

SUBSCRIPTION INFORMATION

In principle annual subscriptions to the series should be taken, but *prepaid* orders of individual issues will also be accepted.
Subscription Price: Hfl. 200,– per calendar-year (8 texts of each ca. 100-130 pp.) + postage.
Individual texts: Hfl. 30,– + postage; prepayment required.

PUBLISHED BY

John Benjamins B. V., Publisher
Amsteldijk 44 – P.O.Box 52519 – The Netherlands
1007 HA AMSTERDAM
Telephone: (020) 73 81 56 – Telex 15798